What to Do When Someone Dies

About the author

Paul Harris is a recently retired manager of a group of funeral directors in the south of England, who is still actively involved in the funeral profession. Before this, he trained as an electronic engineer, and later spent more than 25 years in the Free Church ministry. Here he organised seminars and lectured on many subjects, including bereavement care. He writes for various periodicals, and is a regular broadcaster on matters relating to funerals and bereavement.

Acknowledgements

The author and publisher would like to thank Hilary Fenton-Harris, Healthcare Manager at Poole Hospital NHS Trust, for contributing the chapter on organ donation; Diane Campbell and Robert Macaulay for revising the Scottish sections which were supplied by Michael Scanlan; and Mike Naylor for updating Chapters 20 and 21.

What to Do When Someone Dies

Paul Harris

Which? Books are commissioned by
Consumers' Association and published by
Which? Ltd, 2 Marylebone Road, London NW1 4DF
Email: books@which.co.uk

First edition April 1967
New edition April 1994
Revised edition May 1995
Revised edition March 1997
Reprinted October 1997
Revised edition May 1998
Reprinted June 1999
Revised edition March 2000
Revised edition May 2002
Reprinted February 2003
Revised edition February 2004
Revised edition May 2005

British Library Cataloguing in Publication Data
A catalogue record for *What to Do When Someone Dies* is available from the
British Library

ISBN 1 84490 014 2

For a full list of Which? books, please call 0800 252100, access our website
at www.which.co.uk, or write to Which? Books, Freepost, PO Box 44,
Hertford SG14 1SH.

Editorial and production: Robert Gray, Nithya Rae
Index: Marie Lorimer
Original cover concept by Sarah Harmer
Cover photograph by Steve Satushek/getty images
Typeset by Saxon Graphics Ltd, Derby
Printed and bound in Wales by Creative Print and Design

Contents

★ An asterisk next to the name of an organisation in the text indicates that the address can be found in this section

Foreword

'Whoever wants to read a book about *death*?', asked a friend, some time ago.

Elizabeth Kubler-Ross, pioneer of the hospice system in the USA, described death has 'the last great taboo' – a topic just not discussed, and avoided wherever possible. Events of the last few years have changed that. The shocking terrorist attacks on the USA on 11 September 2001, the war in Iraq in 2003 with countless Iraqi deaths and the rising number of British and American casualties, and the appalling disaster of the earthquake and tsunami in the Indian Ocean on 26 December 2004 have brought the subject of death and bereavement before people's minds in an obstinately persistent manner. The threat of international terrorism has made it clear that nowhere and no one is completely safe. Further, the presentation of television programmes such as *Six Feet Under* have brought the subject before millions of viewers: for these, and many other reasons, the subject of death and dying is much more acceptable than it used to be. Which is as it ought to be. As Benjamin Franklin said, 'In this world, nothing can be said to be certain except death and taxes'.

What Mr Franklin would have made of our present-day taxes is far from certain, and while tax avoidance and tax evasion may release some from the latter, there is no avoiding the universal experience of the former. We are all born, and – sometime – we will all die. Without being morbid, surely it makes sense to make some preparation for this inevitable event? Sooner or later, someone close to us will die, and we may be faced with the responsibility of arranging their funeral. This book shows you how to do this, and how to make reasonable preparations for your own funeral.

Since 1967, this book has helped many thousands of people, by making clear what you *must* do (there is not much of this) and describing what you *may* do (there is rather a lot more of that). It aims to cut through a morass of confusion, and will make it easier for you to decide on the kind of funeral arrangements that you want, pointing out some of the advantages, disadvantages and difficulties you may encounter in the process.

Outline of contents

The book is divided into self-contained chapters, and essential information is duplicated where appropriate to make for easy reference. Essential matters such as obtaining a doctor's certificate and registering a death are clearly explained, and the pros and cons of burial *vs* cremation are outlined. The role of the funeral director – and how to manage without one – is also described, together with the functions of other people with whom you will come into contact: doctors, registrars, ministers, cemetery or crematorium officials, and in some cases, the police and the coroner. All of these will advise and sometimes instruct (or in the case of the coroner, insist) on a particular course of action, but it is generally the executor or nearest relative who has the responsibility of making the necessary decisions. If you have taken on this role, *What to Do When Someone Dies* describes what needs to be done, when, how and with whom to set about it.

This book also advises on humanist and other non-Christian funerals: interest in non-religious funerals has been growing at a steadily increasing rate. Many people now have little contact with the organised church in their life, and feel it hypocritical to expect a church service at the time of their death. Nevertheless, parish priests often like to be informed of any death which occurs in their parish and will be ready to help whether or not the bereaved require religious services.

Following extensive media attention about the retention of human organs following post mortem examinations, new guidelines have now been introduced. There is also a great deal of information readily available, and communication with, and consent from, relatives of those undergoing such examinations is now greatly improved. Chapter 2 gives further information, and more details relating to deaths that occur in hospital.

Chapter 7 provides relevant information about organ donation. While many lives have been saved in the last two years as organs have been donated – not only in death but also in life – there is still a desperate need as many thousands wait for the gift of a life-saving organ. There continues to be growing interest in an opt-out rather than an opt-in system to make organs available, but progress is painfully slow.

The death of close relatives and friends is painful enough when expected, but the experience of sudden and terrible loss plunges us into acute grief, which is made worse when, as in the events of 11 September 2001 and the tsunami disaster, there are no bodies to say goodbye to and grieve over. Chapter 18 provides a brief introduction to the grief process: some of the ways in which death and bereavement affect us personally.

The book also contains a guide to Social Security benefits which may be obtained, including help from the Social Fund towards paying for the funeral (see Chapter 21). Prices are quoted wherever possible, but as many of these change annually or at irregular intervals – sometimes with very little notice – they should be checked carefully in your local area. Always check with your Social Security office (and tax office, where appropriate) to ensure you have up-to-date information. You may lose out if you do not do so.

Although it is impossible within the confines of this book to explore all the details of every relevant area, the list of addresses at the end of the book will lead you to organisations from which further information can be obtained.

Recent developments

During the last few years, an increasing number of people have come to see a funeral service as a celebration of a person's life. Generally, this means that people want a great deal more input into the funeral service, and often a great deal of involvement in it. This is no longer seen as necessarily expensive: a wide range of music is available on CDs, and most crematoria have the means to play such recordings; many homes now have PCs, and many attractive service sheets are produced with considerable artistry and innovation. Certainly, more and more people are becoming cost-conscious where funerals are concerned; while some still want the best 'whatever it costs', many more want to know just what they may be getting from the funeral director for their money.

In July 2001, the Office of Fair Trading (OFT) produced its report on the funeral profession; the findings are referred to in Chapter 8.

The OFT places particular stress on the importance of printed, itemised price lists being produced by funeral directors and made available to customers; while all members of the trade organisations – the NAFD and SAIF (see page 11) – are committed to providing price lists, it is clear that many funeral directors do not.

The OFT report also makes reference to the Charter for the Bereaved, produced in 1996 by the Institute of Burial and Cremation Administration (IBCA – renamed the Institute of Cemetery and Crematorium Management, or ICCM, in September 2003) as a response to the government's Citizen's Charter Initiative. The Charter was produced to improve the experience of funerals for the small but growing number of people who want to dispense with the services of the traditional funeral director, or who would like to become better acquainted with the processes involved. The Charter also encourages burial and funeral authorities to become Charter Members, exhorting them to adhere strictly to a list of rights, which such members will always bring to the attention of their clients.

Charter members increasingly strive to improve environmental efficiency and understanding. The conservation of wildlife and management of burial grounds and crematoria according to sound environmental principles is a matter of growing importance (see Chapter 10).

The number of woodland burial grounds has increased dramatically in the last few years; in 1994 there was only one listed 'green' burial site, now there are over 180. In these, burial takes place as normal, but memorials are usually limited to a shrub or tree (see Chapter 10). While most traditional funeral directors will be able to arrange burial in a woodland burial ground, and provide an environmentally friendly coffin, a recent development has been the emergence of 'green' funeral directors, who deal only with such funerals. Most of the 'green' organisations are keenly aware of the cost factor in funerals, and are eager to reduce them. However, some woodland burial grounds can be quite expensive, and caution should be exercised in purchasing materials and making commitments to services before the costs have been carefully examined.

An increasing number of people continue to set up websites in memory of relatives and friends; two years ago, almost all were American, but now a reasonable number of UK-based bereavement websites exist. These can offer an informal way of remembering someone, and provide much information to those with access to the Internet (see Chapter 16). The presence of these sites has possibly contributed to the dwindling popularity of funeral supermarkets, which provide all the items required for a funeral in one retail outlet.

The incidence of cot deaths has decreased remarkably in the last ten years or so, and details of this will be found in Chapter 19. This is largely due to the tireless work of charitable organisations dedicated to the prevention of infant deaths.

Governmental reports

The Review of Death Certification and Coroner Services was set up in July 2001. After considerable consultation, the review group produced a report in 2003, which recommended significant changes to the procedure of registering deaths and the services of HM Coroner. Details of the report can be found on *www.official-documents.co.uk*; the six major changes can be found in Chapter 3.

The third report of the Shipman Inquiry – the inquiry into the killings by the GP Harold Shipman – published in 2003, also recommended significant changes to the procedure of registering deaths. They are similar to, but not identical with, those suggested by the Coroner's Review. The relevant detail can be found in Chapter 19 of the third report (*www.the-shipman-inquiry.org.uk*).

It appears likely that a common system based on these recommendations will eventually put all death registration into the hands of an expanded and reorganised coroners' system, but it is likely to be some time before this takes place.

The funeral industry

Having changed considerably in recent years, the funeral business continues to evolve now we have entered the twenty-first century. Independent funeral directors, either as a stand-alone business or grouped as small co-operatives, still represent more than 60 per cent of the funerals in the UK. Of the corporate groups, the Co-operative Funeral Services is the largest, supplying about 25 per cent of funerals. Until recently there were several co-operative groups which were almost independent, but a merger brought many of them together under the name of this organisation. The other large group is Dignity Caring Funeral Services (formerly SCI), which carries out approximately 12 per cent of UK funerals.

It is still common practice for the original trading names to be retained when the business has been sold to a conglomerate; however, there is growing emphasis on the necessity for funeral businesses to display their ultimate ownership prominently – a move supported by the OFT. Concerns continue to be expressed over the marketing techniques of some companies, and as in any buying situation, consumers should not allow themselves to be pressurised into buying something that they do not really want and cannot afford.

The National Association of Funeral Directors (NAFD)* brings together the majority of funeral businesses in the UK, including the corporate Co-operative Funeral Services, Dignity Caring Funeral Services and many independent funeral directors. The Society of Allied and Independent Funeral Directors (SAIF)* represents most of the independent funeral businesses in the UK. Both associations have similar codes of practice, and make provision for the handling of complaints and a system of arbitration. Unfortunately, the Funeral Ombudsman Scheme is no longer operative.

It may be that the OFT will reconsider the introduction of compulsory registration for funeral directors. It is incredible to think that anyone, without qualification or experience, can set up and operate as a funeral director. The OFT encourages training, but the funeral business as a whole has been very slow to encourage it; participation in the NVQ on Funeral Directing has been so poor that the qualification has been withdrawn. The NAFD's Diploma in Funeral Directing is an excellent qualification, and this (or something very similar) should surely be seen as the basis for any future registration of businesses. Many people feel strongly that the official regulation of the funeral profession would help to ensure the provision of a professional and caring service, so that no advantage could be taken of bereaved and vulnerable people. A common code of practice between the associations would be a step in the right direction, but much, much more is needed.

Chapter 1

Death

An encounter with death

All of us will, at some time, experience bereavement as a member of the family or a close friend dies. Not all of us, however, will unexpectedly come across someone who appears to be dead, and it is important to know what to do. It can be difficult to tell whether the person you have found really is dead or not; for instance, someone rescued from water may appear not to breathe, yet may be revived by artificial respiration or the 'kiss of life'. The shock of the encounter must not prevent you from trying to find out whether the person is still alive or not. Follow these basic principles:

- make sure it is safe to approach: for instance, is the person touching an electric cable? If so, don't touch him or her – call the emergency services immediately
- check for signs of life by shaking and shouting at the person to try and get a response
- look, listen and feel to check for breathing
- if the person is not breathing, look for other signs of life: check his or her colour and body temperature and try to feel for a pulse. Someone who has been dead for a few hours will be much colder than usual, but a low body temperature alone is not a sure sign of death.

If there is any doubt whether someone is dead, treat him or her as still being alive. Take great care in examining any person found apparently dead out of doors: someone may appear to be dead, but in reality be still alive and suffering from spinal or internal injuries which could prove fatal if he or she were moved.

Telling the doctor

The first thing to do is to call the medical services. The death may have occurred in your own home or that of a friend, or you may have come across someone apparently dead out of doors. Unless the person concerned had been ill and death was partly expected, call the emergency services for an ambulance immediately; if you are out of doors and have a mobile phone, use it. In this situation, when the paramedics arrive and confirm death, the police and coroner will be informed, and the body will be taken to the coroner's mortuary for examination. If, however, the doctor has been in regular attendance, and the person concerned has been expected to die, do not call the emergency services unless there is any doubt at all that death really has occurred. Should a terminally ill person die at home in the middle of the night, there is no need to inform the doctor until early the following morning.

Ask the doctor whether he or she is going to come. If the death has been peaceful and expected, the doctor may not feel it necessary to come, or at least not straight away. If the doctor does not intend coming, ask his or her permission for a funeral director to remove the body, which may not be done otherwise. If a decision has already been made that the funeral will involve cremation, you should tell the doctor at this point as papers will need to be prepared which will involve the doctor examining the body and arranging for another doctor to perform a similar examination. Some doctors make a point of seeing the body of every patient who has died as soon as is convenient. However, the doctor may prefer to examine the deceased at the funeral director's mortuary, in which case (with the doctor's permission) the body may be removed by the appropriate funeral director. If the body is to be kept at home, keep the relevant room as cool as possible by turning off the room heating, keeping the door closed, and, if necessary, leaving a window open. In hot weather it may be advisable to keep the body cool by using cloth-wrapped ice packs.

Laying out the body

The initial preparation of the body for burial or cremation is called **laying out**; if this is done by a nurse or in hospital it will be referred to as 'last offices', while a funeral director will refer to it as 'first offices' (because it is the last service performed for the deceased by the medical profession and the first by the funeral director). This involves washing and tidying the body, closing the eyelids and ensuring that the jaw remains closed. The hair is tidied and sometimes washed, the arms and legs are straightened and, if necessary, the body's orifices are stopped with cotton wool. A man may need to be shaved as the hair continues to grow for some time after death. If laying out is done by a funeral director, the body will be dressed ready for the funeral, either in a funeral gown or, if preferred by the relatives, in everyday clothes.

There is a small but growing tendency for the family to arrange and conduct funerals for deceased relatives – see 'Arranging a funeral without a funeral director', Chapter 15. In this case, you can do the laying out yourself at home. Most people still prefer to hand over funeral arrangements to a funeral director, who will then attend to the laying out. This may be done at home, if preferred; a funeral director will not normally charge extra for this service within working hours, but will usually prefer to attend to the deceased at his or her mortuary. Many hospitals now provide only a basic laying out service, leaving the majority to be done by the funeral director.

Rigor mortis is a stiffening of the muscles, which usually begins within about six hours after death and gradually extends over the whole body in about 24 hours; after this it usually begins to wear off. Rigor mortis is less pronounced in the body of an elderly person.

When someone has been dead for half an hour or more, parts of the skin often begin to discolour with purple/black patches. This is called **hypostasis**, or post mortem (meaning 'after death' – nothing to do with post mortem examinations) staining, and is due to blood settling in parts of the body due to the action of gravity.

If someone has died at home in bed, quietly and expectedly, it is perfectly in order to rearrange the body and tidy the room. If, however, someone collapses and dies unexpectedly, or a dead body is discovered in unusual circumstances, you must summon an ambulance immediately and do as little as possible until it comes. Do not move the body unless there are exceptional circumstances, for example, if someone collapses and dies while crossing a road or at the top of a flight of stairs.

Calling the police

If you think that death appears to have been caused by an accident or violence, or to have occurred in other non-natural or suspicious circumstances, you must inform the police at once. The police will inform the coroner.

Do not touch or move anything in the room, or allow anyone else to do so, until the police say that you may. The police will almost certainly want to take statements from anyone who was with the deceased when he or she died, or who discovered the body, but no one is obliged to give a statement to the police. If there is an inquest later, anyone who has made a statement may be called as a witness, as may any person whom the coroner believes may be able to give information about the death.

If a body cannot be identified immediately, the police circulate a description in police journals, and occasionally to the general press, too. Anyone who might be able to identify the body usually has to go to the mortuary with the police.

If the police are called and no relative or other person responsible is immediately available, the police take possession of any cash or valuables. As a general rule, this property is given up to whomever can later prove the right to it. The police also take away any article which may have a bearing on the cause of death – a letter or bottle of pills, for example – in case this is needed by the coroner.

Medical certificate of the cause of death

Every death that occurs in the UK must be registered at the local registrar's office within five days (see Chapter 3) and the registrar will require a certificate providing medical evidence of the cause of death. Normally, the doctor who has been attending the deceased will sign the certificate, but he or she cannot do so if there is any doubt whatsoever about the actual cause of death.

If the doctor knows the cause of death, he or she will provide the relatives with a certificate which states (to the best of the doctor's knowledge) the cause or causes of death, the last date on which he or she saw the patient alive and whether or not a doctor has seen the body since death occurred. This will usually be given to the family in a sealed envelope, together with a small form which gives basic details about registering the death. No charge is made for the certificate.

If the doctor is uncertain for any reason about the actual cause of death or has not seen the patient within a period of 14 days before death occurred (28 days in Northern Ireland), he or she cannot sign the death certificate. In such cases the coroner must be informed (see Chapter 6) – the coroner's officer will normally contact the family and explain procedures. The body will then be taken to the coroner's mortuary (usually at a local hospital) where the cause of death will be investigated, which may or may not involve a post mortem examination. In such cases, the period for registration may be extended as long as the registrar is informed of the circumstances so that appropriate action can be taken. The relatives arranging the funeral should do this.

In normal cases where the doctor signs the medical certificate of the cause of death, this must be used to register the death at the register office in the district or sub-district in which the death occurred. However, in England and Wales information may be given at any other register office, if this is more convenient. This will then be passed on to the register office in the sub-district where the death occurred (see Chapter 3).

Chapter 2

Death in hospital

The great majority of deaths in urban areas now occur in hospitals or nursing homes. When someone dies in a hospital or similar institution, the course of events up to when the death is registered is slightly different from the way that arrangements are made if the death occurred at home.

Most nursing staff usually have a good idea of when a patient is likely to die, and will call relatives to the hospital if they are not already there so that they may be present when the death occurs. If this is not possible, the relatives, or whoever was named as next of kin when the patient was admitted, will be informed of the death by the ward nursing staff, or the hospital's bereavement officer. Sometimes, the person who died may not be an in-patient at the hospital, but may die while attending the Accident and Emergency department, or an outpatients clinic. In such cases, a member of the family will probably be asked to identify the body.

If death was unexpected, the result of an accident, or occurred during an operation or while the patient was recovering from an anaesthetic, the coroner must be informed and will investigate the cause of death (see page 21). Normally, all deaths taking place within 24 hours of an operation or admission to the hospital will be reported to the coroner. This so-called '24-hour admission rule' is not a statutory requirement, but many coroners require such referrals to be made as a matter of course, with a view to ensuring that a death which may be due to unnatural causes is not missed.

Contact with the hospital

All hospitals have considerable experience of dealing with bereaved relatives, and the staff appointed to this duty are usually patient and sympathetic. However, demands on nurses' and doctors' time are considerable, and emergencies often arise; it is thus likely that, from time to time, some waiting may be involved. The hospital will do its best to make its procedures clear, and most now publish bereavement booklets which contain essential information for bereaved relatives.

If a death occurs in the evening or the middle of the night, the body of the deceased person will be moved to the hospital mortuary, and an appointment made with the relatives to deal with the formalities on the following day. The deceased's possessions will have to be removed from the hospital, and these can usually be collected from the hospital's property office by the next of kin or his or her authorised representative. A letter of authorisation may be necessary, and a signature will be required.

If the medical certificate of the cause of death can be issued at the hospital, the relatives of the deceased person will have to arrange for his or her body to be collected from the hospital mortuary. This may be done through a funeral director or by the relatives or friends.

Making arrangements with a funeral director

Most people consult a funeral director to make arrangements for the funeral (but see Chapter 15 for funerals without a funeral director), and he or she will arrange for the removal of the body of the deceased from the hospital. The hospital will not recommend any particular funeral director, but will usually be able to supply a list of funeral directors in the local area. Some hospitals now provide a short list of approved funeral directors; more may do so when funeral directors' Codes of Practice are seen to conform with the new regime required by the Office of Fair Trading (OFT), and eventually receive the OFT's stamp of approval. At the time of writing, both funeral trades associations have applied for this. The National Funerals College* currently recommends that hospitals, hospices and nursing and residential homes should appoint an independent funeral adviser to provide advice and practical help to those who need it. The OFT supports this suggestion, and also recommends the inclusion of certain essential information in hospital literature for the newly bereaved. For information about finding a funeral director online, see page 133.

The funeral director concerned should be informed of the situation promptly; most operate a 24-hour emergency service, but there is no need to inform him or her of a death that occurs in the middle of the night until the next morning. Most hospital mortuaries are not open for public business until 9 am, and in cases where the funeral involves cremation, time must be allowed for the necessary papers to be prepared. This will sometimes involve a delay of up to 48 hours – maybe longer if a weekend is included. There is a charge for these forms, which is set annually by the British Medical Association; this is usually paid by the funeral director, and the amount added to the funeral account.

The next of kin or executor will usually have to sign a form authorising the removal of the body to the funeral director's premises.

Making your own funeral arrangements

Those who wish to collect the body of a deceased relative or friend themselves should find out when the hospital mortuary is open for such services, as most now restrict the times when bodies may be removed. If the relatives have decided to carry out funeral arrangements themselves, they must come to the hospital mortuary at an appointed time bringing with them either a suitable coffin or a stretcher, enough people to carry it, and a vehicle long enough to convey it. New Health and Safety guidelines now discourage mortuary staff from assisting with placing the body in a coffin or on a stretcher, or helping to load it on the vehicle.

Hospital funeral arrangements

If a person who dies in a hospital or NHS community care home has no relatives or friends to arrange and pay for his or her funeral, NHS trusts undertake a similar role to that of local authorities in arranging a funeral. Guidance was published in 1997 on minimum standards for the funerals of such patients where the NHS trust takes responsibility. Hospitals will generally endeavour to find out whether the patient had a preference for burial or cremation, and will attempt to search for relatives or friends.

If there has been a church connection, the local incumbent will be involved; otherwise the hospital chaplain will become responsible for the funeral service. Most hospitals have arrangements with local funeral directors to provide such funeral services.

Medical certificate of the cause of death

In the great majority of cases, the cause of death is known to be due to natural causes. In these circumstances a hospital doctor fills out a form indicating the cause of death, and this is given to the next of kin. Hospital procedures differ, but it is usually the administrative rather than the medical staff who provide the medical certificate of the cause of death, and make arrangements with the relatives for the patient's belongings to be collected.

If the person died before a hospital doctor had a chance to diagnose the cause, then the deceased patient's own doctor may be asked to issue the death certificate. However, if the GP feels that there is reasonable doubt as to the cause of death, he or she will be unable to sign the certificate, and the matter will be referred to the coroner. When the coroner is involved, it will not be possible for a doctor to issue a medical certificate of the cause of death (see Chapter 6), unless the coroner's consultations with the hospital and/or the patient's GP show beyond any reasonable doubt that the patient died from natural causes. In such cases a post mortem examination will not normally be required, and the death certificate will be completed as normal and given to the next of kin.

Normally, the medical certificate of the cause of death contains the information required by the registrar in order to register the death (see Chapter 3). This is provided in a sealed envelope with a form which tells the relatives what information the registrar will require from them. If the coroner becomes involved, there will be no medical certificate of the cause of death, but the coroner will provide the register office with the necessary information. Registration will not be possible and funeral arrangements cannot be finalised until the registrar has received the necessary documents from the coroner.

Registration

The procedure for registering a death in hospital is the same as that for a death which occurred at home (see Chapter 3), but the death must be registered at the register office in the same registration district where the hospital is situated. If that same registration district or sub-district has another office or out-station which is nearer and therefore more convenient for the relatives of the deceased, registration may be carried out there. Further information regarding the registration (see Chapter 3) may be given at any register office in England and Wales for transmission to the correct registration district. For deaths which take place in Scotland, see Chapter 4.

Involvement of the coroner

It is the coroner's responsibility to discover the cause of death, and in order to do this he or she may arrange for a post mortem examination to be held (Section 19[1] of the Coroner's Act 1988). These coroners' post mortems are required by law in England, Wales and Northern Ireland, and do not require the agreement or consent of relatives.

The coroner will normally require a post-mortem to be carried out in order to investigate:

- sudden and unexpected death
- death where the cause of death is uncertain, and the doctor cannot issue a death certificate
- death where the cause of death is known or suspected to be due to causes other than natural disease, such as accidents and industrial disease
- death which may be due to medical mishap
- death due to violence, neglect, abortion, or any kind of poisoning.

Once the coroner becomes involved, the responsibility for the body lies with the coroner's office rather than with the hospital. The coroner, through his or her coroner's officer, will then provide relatives with the necessary information; the hospital will tell the relatives how to contact the coroner's office. The government's review on the work of the Coroner Services has recommended

21

changes to this procedure, but none of these is in force at the time this book went to print, nor are likely to be implemented in the immediate future.

Post mortem examinations

There are two types of post mortem examination:

- the **coroner's post mortem**, which is required by law where death cannot clearly be seen to be due to natural causes. This is a statutory requirement, and the consent and agreement of relatives is not required. Relatives will not automatically be told the results of the post mortem, and should ask for the results if they want to know.
- the **hospital (or 'consented') post mortem**, which is usually carried out at the request of the doctors who have been caring for the deceased person, or sometimes at the request of close relatives who want to find out more about the cause of death of a family member. This is a post mortem requiring the consent of the relatives, and can be carried out only when written agreement has been obtained. If relatives agree to a hospital post mortem, the doctors will normally issue the medical certificate of the cause of death before the examination takes place, so that funeral arrangements can proceed.

Hospital post mortems

Hospital post mortems can be either:

- **full** This involves a detailed examination of all the internal organs including the brain, heart, lungs, liver, kidneys, intestines, blood vessels and small glands. These are removed from the body, examined in detail and then returned to the body; or
- **limited** For those who are uncomfortable about agreeing to a full post mortem, a limited post mortem may be carried out. This involves examination only of those organs directly connected with the patient's last illness; the pathologist will examine only the organs about which agreement has been reached. This may limit the usefulness of the examination, and mean that no information will be available about possible abnormalities present in other organs, but which may have contributed to the patient's death.

Hospitals wanting to carry out such post mortem examinations should now obtain clear and detailed consent from families of the deceased, under new guidelines issued by the Chief Medical Officer in April 2003. A number of hospitals now produce booklets on post mortem examinations for relatives, which are available on request.

Under some circumstances, relatives may be asked if they have any objection to the use of the organs of the deceased person for transplant surgery. Even if the patient had completed a donor card and enrolled on the NHS Organ Donor Register*, the relatives will be consulted before any organs are removed (see Chapter 7).

Organ and tissue retention

Pathologists who carry out a post mortem may request the retention of specific organs or tissue samples in order to enable medical staff to carry out a more detailed examination. The reasons for this may include:

- determination of the cause of death
- specific current research projects
- future examination as new diagnostic techniques or fresh knowledge become available
- the education and training of medical students and doctors
- discussions between other pathologists.

In all these ways, the retention of organs and tissue blocks can benefit not only the relatives of the deceased but also the wider community, by improving diagnosis, treatment and the understanding of health problems.

Following a coroner's post mortem, material must be retained for as long as it has any bearing on ascertaining the cause of death; this includes sorting out any legal proceedings relating to the death. In practice, items are often retained after the coroner is satisfied for the reasons given above. Concern following recent problems with organ retention means that the legal framework for this practice is now being reviewed, to clarify when material should be kept and for how long. When a hospital post mortem is carried out, the permission of the next of kin must be obtained before any organs or tissue blocks are retained.

New guidelines on retention of material

Great anxiety and concern was expressed by many after it was revealed that a number of hospitals had retained certain organs and tissue samples, removed at post mortem examinations, without the knowledge or consent of the next of kin. Because of this, new guidelines for hospital post mortems were issued in 2000, which are being constantly reviewed; the latest code of practice, *Families and Post Mortems*, was published in April 2003, and is available from the Department of Health. These guidelines make it clear to relatives that accurate information will be given to them at all times, and that their permission will be sought before the retention of any organs or tissue samples required for further research or investigation. To assist relatives, the new guidance on post mortem practice includes a video called *Respect for the Dead* (September 2004) and examples of the new consent forms produced by the Royal College of Pathologists. Guidance about clear communication applies both to post mortem examinations ordered by the coroner, and to those agreed on between families and hospitals.

These and other similar materials are available from Department of Health Publications*.

Disposal of retained material

Organs, tissue blocks (small squares of chemically treated tissue) and slides that have been retained are now required to be returned for respectful disposal if relatives want this, but the large size of many hospital archives means that checking them all takes a long time. Relatives may agree that hospitals can continue to keep such material for future use in order to benefit other patients, or ask the hospital to dispose respectfully of the organs, blocks and slides. A helpful booklet entitled *Tissue Blocks and Slides* was produced by the Retained Organs Commission. The Commission ceased to operate in March 2004, but this and other publications can be obtained from the Department of Health Publications*. The Commission's website* is currently still available for reference, but is likely to be deleted by the end of 2005.

Chapter 3

Registering the death

In England and Wales, a death should be registered within five days of its happening. Registration can be delayed for a further nine days provided the registrar receives, in writing, confirmation that a medical certificate of the cause of death has been signed by the doctor.

Where to register

Under English law, all deaths must be registered in the registration sub-district in which they took place or in which the body was found (the 'receiving registrar'). However, if it is more convenient the information required may be taken to any register office in England and Wales (*not* Scotland or Northern Ireland) – the 'attesting registrar' – from which it will be passed on to the relevant register office.

A list of names, addresses and telephone numbers of local registrars of births and deaths is usually displayed in doctors' surgeries and in public libraries and other public buildings, together with their office hours and a description of the sub-district they cover.

Usually, whoever is giving the information goes in person to the registrar's office. An increasing number of registration districts now operate on an appointments system, although it is usually possible for you just to go along during the registrar's office hours and wait until he or she is free to see you.

Who can register a death?

Only some people are qualified by law to inform the registrar of the details of the death which has occurred.

If the death has occurred inside a house or public building, any of the following (in order of precedence) may register the death:

- a relative of the deceased who was present at the death
- a relative of the deceased who was present during the last illness
- a relative of the deceased who was not present at the death or during the last illness but who lives in the district or sub-district where the death occurred
- a person who is not a relative but who was present at the time of death
- the occupier (e.g. the matron of a nursing home or warden of pensioners' flats) of the building where the death occurred, if he or she was aware of the details of the death
- the person arranging for the disposal of the body (this means the person accepting responsibility for the funeral – *not* the funeral director, who is not normally allowed to register the death).

If the person has been found dead elsewhere, the following are qualified to register the death:

- any relative of the deceased able to provide the registrar with the required details
- any person present at the time of death
- the person who found the body
- the person in charge of the body (which will be the police if the body cannot be identified)
- the person accepting responsibility for arranging the funeral.

The person who registers the death is known as 'the informant'. The responsibility cannot be delegated to a person who is not qualified to act as informant: should such a person attend the register office, the registrar will refuse to register the death and will require a qualified informant to attend.

In cases where a coroner's inquest has been held, the coroner will act as the informant and provide the registrar with all the necessary details. In this case there is no need for the family and relatives to register the death, although they will need to attend the register office if copies of the death certificate are needed, or arrange for them to be sent by post.

What information is required

The registrar will require the following information:

- the date and place of death
- the full name and surname of the deceased (and the maiden name if the deceased was a married woman)
- the date and place of birth of the deceased
- the occupation of the deceased (and husband's name and occupation if the deceased was a married woman or widow)
- the usual address of the deceased
- whether the deceased was in receipt of a pension or allowance from public funds
- if the deceased was married, the date of birth of the surviving partner.

The medical certificate of the cause of death states that the deceased's National Health Service medical card should be taken and given to the registrar. However, if this cannot be found, registration should not be delayed: provision of the card is no longer a strict necessity.

The medical certificate

The medical certificate of the cause of death must be submitted to the receiving registrar: if this is taken to the attesting registrar, it will be sent with other information by first-class post to the receiving registrar, who must receive it before the death can be registered. Time for this must be allowed: it is wise not to fix a date for the funeral until at least one week after giving information to the attesting registrar.

The doctor who completes the medical certificate must also fill in that part of it which provides information for the informant. One side of the certificate is entitled 'notice to informant' and provides details of the information required by the registrar; the other lists those who are qualified to act as informants. In some cases, the doctor or hospital may send the medical certificate of the cause of death direct to the registrar, or via a funeral director; this and the information from the attesting registrar must be received by the receiving registrar before the death can be registered. Again, it is important to allow sufficient time for processing and possible postal delays if the funeral is to take place as planned.

If the registrar finds that the information the doctor has given on the medical certificate of the cause of death is inadequate or that the death was due to some cause that should have been reported to the coroner, he or she must inform the coroner accordingly and await written clearance before proceeding with the registration. He or she must also inform the coroner if it is found that the doctor had not seen the deceased within 14 days prior to death or after death.

The registration procedure

The procedure for registering a death is a simple question-and-answer interview between the registrar and the informant.

The registrar will, first of all, make sure that the death took place in his or her sub-district; a death cannot be registered if it occurred in any place outside the registrar's sub-district. He or she will ask in what capacity whoever is registering the death qualifies to be the informant – relative, present at the death, or other reason. The registrar may ask if the informant has brought the deceased's birth certificate and marriage certificate, and National Health Service medical card. It is not essential for the informant to have these, but they contain some of the information the registrar will need.

Then the registrar fills in a draft form for the register of deaths with the date of death and exactly where it occurred, the sex, names and surname of the dead person. It is as well to give all the names by which the deceased has ever been known, so that there can be no doubt as to whom the particulars refer. In order to avoid difficulties over identity in connection with probate, insurance policies, pensions and bank accounts, the names should be the same as those on birth and marriage certificates, and on any other relevant documents. The maiden surname of a married woman is required. The date and place of birth of the dead person, and last address, are entered. For someone who died away from home, the home address should be given.

Next, the registrar will want to know the last full-time occupation of the deceased, and whether he or she was retired at the time of death. A woman who was married or widowed at the time of her death would be described as 'wife of' or 'widow of', followed by the name and occupation of her husband, in addition to her own occupation or profession. A woman who had never been married or a woman whose marriage had been dissolved would have her occupation recorded, with no reference to her marital status.

Children under the age of 16 are described as 'son of' or 'daughter of', followed by the names and occupations of the parents.

The registrar copies the medical cause of death from the doctor's certificate or the coroner's notification, and adds the name and qualification of the doctor or coroner.

On the draft form, but not in the register itself, the registrar enters the deceased's National Health Service number. If the deceased was over 16 years old, additional information is requested: marital status at the time of death (single, married, widowed or divorced) and the date of birth of any widow or widower left. This information is not entered in the register in England and Wales, and is used only for the preparation of population statistics by the Registrar General.

Entry in the register

Many register offices are now computerised; it is likely that your information about the deceased will be entered into a computer system and your copy, or copies, of the death certificate produced by a computer printer. Note that you will still be required to sign the register in the usual way.

The informant should check the draft of the proposed entry in the register to make sure that there is nothing wrong or misleading in it. When the particulars are agreed, the registrar makes the entry in the register itself and asks the informant to check and sign it. The informant should sign his or her usual signature. The registrar has to use special ink for the register, so sign with the pen offered.

After adding the date of the registration, the registrar signs the entry in the final space. Any errors can be corrected without formality before the entry has been signed, but once it is signed by the registrar, the entry cannot be corrected without documentary evidence to justify the correction. Some errors cannot be corrected without authorisation from the Registrar General. The registrar can now let you have copies of the entry in the register (the death certificates), which you may need for probate and other purposes. In addition to the copies of the death certificate, the registrar will provide, without charge, a copy of a form for Social Security purposes, and a green certificate for the funeral director or other person arranging the funeral, authorising the funeral to take place.

Make a note of the number of the entry in the register and the date, and also note the registration district, because you may need more copies of the entry later. Copies of entries in the current register cost £3.50 (2005), increasing to £7 once the register is in the custody of the Superintendent Registrar. If, subsequently, details of the registration and registration district are lost, application for a search must be made to the Public Search Room*, and the fee for a copy of the entry made in this way is £11.50 (2005). The fee reduces to £8.50 (2005) if the original reference number is known.

Certificates are now available online, following registration; the fees are the same as they are for certificates ordered by post. A priority service, under which death certificates are despatched the following working day, costs £27.50 if ordered by post. If the reference number is known, the fees come down to £24.50 if ordered by post or phone, or £23 if ordered online (see page 41).

Issue of green certificate for burial or cremation

Once a death has been registered, the registrar issues a green certificate, referred to generally as the disposal certificate, authorising either burial or application for cremation. A body may not be buried or cremated without this certificate or its equivalent – the coroner's order for burial or certificate for cremation. It is unwise to make more than provisional arrangements for the funeral until you have the certificate from either the registrar or the coroner. (See also page 40.)

The registrar can issue a certificate before registering a death, but only when he or she has already received the requisite information (including medical evidence) and is just waiting for the informant to register the death – for instance, when the only suitable informant is ill in hospital but the funeral has to take place. A certificate issued by the registrar before registration authorises burial only; crematorium authorities are not allowed to accept such a certificate.

When you obtain the necessary certificate from the registrar or coroner, you should give it to the funeral director who will take it to the church, cemetery or crematorium officials. Without it, they will not bury or cremate a body. It is the responsibility of the church, cemetery or crematorium to complete Part C of the certificate and to return it to the registrar confirming disposal has taken place. If the registrar does not receive Part C within 14 days of the issue of the certificate, he or she will get in touch with the person to whom the certificate had been given.

Documents for registration

Document	Source	Function	Recipient
notice to informant	doctor	gives details of who must register death and what particulars will be required	via relative to registrar
medical certificate of cause of death	doctor	states cause of death	to registrar (direct or via relative)
If coroner involved: coroner's notification	coroner	confirms or gives details of cause of death	to registrar (direct or via relative)
or coroner's certificate after inquest	coroner	gives all the particulars required for death to be registered	direct to registrar

Registering a stillbirth

In the case of a stillbirth both birth and death need to be registered, a single operation which has to be done within 42 days.

People qualified to register a stillbirth are (as for live births): the mother; the father if the child would have been legitimate had it been born alive; the occupier of the house or other premises in which the stillbirth occurred; a person who was present at the stillbirth or who found the stillborn child.

A stillborn child is a child born after the 24th week of pregnancy which did not at any time after being completely delivered from its mother breathe or show any other signs of life.

If a doctor was in attendance at a stillbirth or examined the body of the stillborn child, he or she can issue a certificate of stillbirth, stating the cause of stillbirth and the duration of the pregnancy. A certified midwife can also issue the certificate if no doctor was there. If no doctor or midwife was in attendance at, or after, the birth, one of the parents, or some other qualified informant, can make a declaration on a form (**Form 35**, available from the registrar of births and deaths), saying that to the best of his or her knowledge and belief the child was stillborn.

If there is any doubt whether the child was born alive or not, the case must be reported to the coroner of the district, who may then order a post mortem or an inquest and will issue a certificate of the cause of death when the inquiries are complete.

When registering a stillbirth, the registrar has to have the doctor's or midwife's certificate, or a declaration of the stillbirth. Whoever goes to register has to tell the registrar of the name of the child where given, the name, surname and maiden name of the mother, her place of birth and her usual residence at the time of the child's birth; if she had never been married, her occupation is also required. If the child would have been legitimate, the name, surname and occupation of the father and his place of birth are required.

If the parents are not married at the time of their baby's birth but do still want the father's details entered, they should ask the registrar to guide them through the rather more involved procedures.

If the father and mother are married to each other, the registrar asks the month and year of the marriage, and the number of the mother's previous children, both born alive and stillborn, by her present and any former husband; this information is needed for statistical purposes only and is not entered in the register.

A certified copy of the stillbirth entry (death certificate) is now obtainable, costing £3.50, although a certificate of registration will be provided free of charge to the informant if it is requested.

Loss of the foetus before the 24th week does not fall within the legal definition of a stillbirth and is usually considered a miscarriage. If the mother was in hospital at the time, the hospital may offer to arrange for the disposal of the remains. But if the parent(s) would like these to be buried or cremated in the usual way, it should be possible to arrange this with a local cemetery or crematorium, provided a form of medical certificate is completed.

Most crematoria make minimal charges for the funerals of stillborn or miscarried children and many funeral directors will provide their services on such occasions free of charge. This means that they will probably not charge for their professional services but will be obliged to pass on any fees for crematoria and so on that they may incur on behalf of their clients. Some hospitals now offer 'reverent disposal' of stillborn and miscarried children, which often involves a simple ceremony led by the hospital chaplain. It should be noted that in such cases there may be no ashes produced for subsequent burial or scattering. See also Chapter 19.

Recent developments

Two important government reviews have recently taken place. The third report of the Shipman Inquiry is now available, and the Review of Death Certification and Coroner Services was published in June 2003. Both recommend substantial changes to the procedure for registering deaths. The recommendations differ in detail, but are broadly similar. They are currently being studied, and have not been implemented to date. Indeed, it does not seem likely that they will be put in place in the immediate future. However, it is probable that eventually registration of death will be dealt with by a reformed and expanded Coroner's Service.

Chapter 4

Registration in Scotland

The medical certificate of the cause of death given by doctors in Scotland is similar to that in England. The obligation to give the certificate rests on the doctor who attended the deceased during the last illness, but, if there was no doctor in attendance, the certificate may be issued by any doctor who is able to do so. The doctor hands the certificate to a relative to take to the local registrar or sends it direct to the registrar. In the majority of cases, the certificate is issued to a relative.

If a medical certificate of cause of death cannot be given, the registrar can, nevertheless, register the death but must report the facts of the case to the procurator fiscal.

The procurator fiscal

There are no coroners in Scotland and the duties which in England would be carried out by a coroner are in Scotland carried out by a procurator fiscal (a full-time law officer, who comes under the authority of the Lord Advocate).

The procurator fiscal has many functions, including responsibility for investigating all sudden, unexpected and violent deaths and also any death which occurred under suspicious circumstances. If satisfied with the doctor's medical certificate and any evidence received from the police, he or she need take no further action. If, however, the procurator fiscal considers a further medical report is necessary, a medical practitioner (frequently a police surgeon) will be requested to report 'on soul and conscience' what he or she considers was the cause of death.

Post mortem

The procurator fiscal will decide whether or not a post mortem is necessary. In the majority of cases, a post mortem is not carried out and the doctor certifies the cause of death after an external examination. The mere fact that the cause of death is in a medical sense unexplained is not a ground for ordering a dissection at public expense, provided the intrinsic circumstances explain sufficiently the cause of death in a popular sense and do not raise a suspicion of criminality or negligence.

If a post mortem is carried out, one doctor is usually sufficient but if, while conducting the dissection, the doctor finds unexpected difficulties, the procurator fiscal may decide to bring in a second doctor. Where there is a possibility of criminal proceedings being taken against someone and it is necessary to prove the fact and cause of death, or where the death is drugs-related, a post mortem should be carried out by two medical practitioners.

Public inquiry

Death while in legal custody or as the result of an accident during work must be the subject of a public inquiry (called a Fatal Accident Inquiry or FAI), which takes the place of an inquest in England. If a person, while engaged in industrial employment or occupation, died of natural causes, there may, but will not necessarily, be a public inquiry.

The procurator fiscal has to report certain cases to the Crown Office and it is the Lord Advocate who makes the final decision about whether to apply to a sheriff for an inquiry to be held. In all other cases, investigations made into sudden deaths are carried out by the procurator fiscal confidentially.

Before reporting a case to the Crown Office, the procurator fiscal may interview witnesses and the relatives in private (this is called a precognition).

Cases which are reported to the Crown Office because they may result in a public inquiry are essentially those involving a matter of the public interest – for instance, to prevent a recurrence of similar circumstances. Deaths which are directly or indirectly connected with the action of a third party, such as road traffic deaths, may be reported to the Crown Office for consideration either of criminal proceedings or of a public inquiry.

A public inquiry is heard before the sheriff in the local sheriff court. The procurator fiscal and the representatives of any other interested parties examine the witnesses but it is the sheriff who determines the circumstances of the death.

When the inquiry is completed, the procurator fiscal notifies the result of the findings to the Registrar General. If the death has already been registered, the Registrar General lets the local registrar know if any changes need to be made to the entry. If the death has not already been registered, the Registrar General instructs the registrar of the district in which the death occurred to register the death.

Registering the death

In Scotland the law requires that every death must be registered within eight days from the date of death.

The person qualified to act as informant for registering a death is any relative of the deceased, any person present at the death, the deceased's executor or other legal representative, the occupier of the premises where the death took place, or any person having knowledge of the particulars to be registered.

Whereas in England a death must be registered in the registration office for the district in which the death occurred, in Scotland the death may be registered either in the office for the district in which the death occurred or in the office for the district in which the deceased had normally resided before the death, provided this was also in Scotland. The death of a visitor to Scotland must be registered where the death took place.

As in England, the procedure for registering a death is a simple question-and-answer interview between registrar and informant. The registrar will request the production of a medical certificate of cause of death or, failing that, the name and address of a doctor who can be asked to give the certificate. The information required by a Scottish registrar to register a death is much the same as in England and Wales, except that he or she also needs to know the time of death; if the deceased had ever been married, the name, surname and occupation of each spouse and date of birth of the surviving spouse; and the name and occupation of the deceased's father and the name, occupation and maiden name of the mother, and whether the parents are alive or dead.

When the form of particulars has been completed, the registrar asks the informant to read it over carefully to ensure that all the particulars are correct and, if a manual registration system is in use, to sign it. (Most registrars' systems are now computerised and it is not necessary to sign. The details of the death will be entered on the computer and the informant will be able to verify these details.) The registrar then makes the entry in the register and asks the informant to check it carefully. The registrar will then also sign the entry.

Registering a stillbirth

A stillbirth in Scotland must be registered within 21 days. As in England, if no doctor or midwife can issue a certificate of stillbirth, an informant must make a declaration on a special form. In Scotland this is **Form 7**, obtainable from the registrar. All such cases, and any case where there is doubt as to whether the child was alive or not, are reported to the procurator fiscal, who notifies the Registrar General of the results of his or her investigations.

If the body is to be cremated, a certificate of stillbirth must be given by the doctor who was in attendance at the confinement (or who conducted a post mortem). The stillbirth must have been registered before cremation can take place.

A stillbirth can be registered either in the district in which it took place or in the district in Scotland in which the mother of the stillborn child was ordinarily resident at the time of the stillbirth.

The informant must produce for the registrar a doctor's or midwife's certificate, or the completed Form 7, and is required to give the same information as in England (see pages 31–3) and, in addition, the time of the stillbirth and, where applicable, the place of the parents' marriage.

Certificate of registration

There is no direct equivalent in Scotland of a disposal certificate (see pages 30–1). After registration, the registrar issues to the informant a certificate of registration of death (**Form 14**), which should be given to the funeral director to give to the keeper of the burial ground or to the crematorium authorities. There is no charge for this certificate.

Death certificates

As in England, the registrar issues, free of charge, a registration or notification of death form which can be used for National Insurance and Social Security purposes. All other death certificates must be paid for.

Death certificates (a full copy of an entry in the death register, sometimes called an extract) are always obtainable from the registrar of the district where the death was registered and cost £8.50 at the time of registration and £13.50 if obtained outwith the year of registration. It is usual to order death certificates/extracts when registering the death.

Chapter 5

After registration

In order to make certain necessary arrangements regarding the deceased's legal and financial affairs, one or more death certificates will almost certainly be needed. These are not the same as the medical certificate of the cause of death signed by a doctor at the time of death, but are certified copies of the entry in the Register of Deaths (the 'standard' death certificate). One certificate each will be needed to apply for probate or letters of administration (see Chapter 20), for dealing with the deceased's bank account, and for claims on insurance policies. Each will cost £3.50 (2005, although the cost is likely to increase at irregular intervals) if obtained at the time of registration or within a few weeks afterwards.

If advice is needed about the number and type of certificates required, a list of the purposes for which evidence of death may be required should be taken to the registrar, who will advise accordingly. New death certificates are printed on heavily watermarked paper, and photocopying these is a breach of copyright. However, individuals or organisations may take copies of death certificates for their own record-keeping purposes, provided that the copies are not passed on to others as evidence of the death.

Notifying the Department for Work and Pensions

The Department for Work and Pensions (DWP)★ must be informed about the death in order to deal with pensions and so on; the registrar will provide a free form (**BD8**) for this purpose – this form should also be used to claim various Social Security benefits after someone has died, but it cannot be used to apply to the Social Fund for help with the cost of the funeral. For this, a different form (**SF200**) is needed, which can be obtained from the local Social

Security office. The funeral director who is dealing with the funeral arrangements may also keep copies, and will assist with completing them and submitting them to one of the Social Security offices which now deal with them (a pre-paid envelope is normally supplied with the form, or the form may be taken to any Social Security office).

There is no longer any form of general death grant; this was abolished some years ago.

Registrar's certificate for burial or cremation

Together with copies of the death certificate and Social Security form BD8, the registrar will provide a green certificate (previously known as the 'disposal certificate'), to say that the death has been registered and that a funeral may take place. Before issuing this certificate, the registrar must have a properly completed medical certificate of the cause of death signed by a doctor. The registrar's green certificate permits burial or cremation to take place and must be given to the funeral director: the funeral cannot take place without it. If the funeral is being organised by the relatives and/or friends themselves, the certificate must be given to the relevant burial or cremation authority. Should the registrar find that there are inaccuracies in the medical certificate of the cause of death, he or she must report this to the Coroner, and registration will have to be deferred until the Coroner is satisfied that everything is in order. In all cases where the Coroner is involved, a different legal process is involved (see Chapter 6).

If the informant is unable to attend the registrar's office within the five days required for notification, the registrar, provided he or she has received a medical certificate of cause of death from the doctor, may issue a certificate for burial, but *not* for cremation.

Careful examination of the registrar's green certificate will show whether it has been issued before or after the informant has registered the death: if it states that it was issued *before* registration, it is suitable for burial only, but if issued *after* registration it is suitable for burial or cremation.

This registrar's certificate must be sent or taken to the cemetery authority or vicar of the churchyard where burial is to take place, or to the office of the local crematorium in the case of cremation. Normally the funeral director will attend to this.

Obtaining death certificates at a later date

Further copies of death certificates may be obtained from the registrar who registered the death while the current volume of the death register remains in use. This is likely to be about one month, but the time varies according to how many deaths are registered each week and whether the death in question was entered near the beginning or end of the relevant register.

When completed, each death register is passed to the Superintendent Registrar of the district, from whom copies of the death certificate can be obtained later if required. The charge for each certificate in this case is £7 (2005).

Applications for certificates by post or online can be made to the General Register Office★. The charge for this is £11.50, but if the index number on a previously issued certificate is known and quoted, the fee is reduced to £8.50 if ordered by post, or £7 online. If all details of a previously issued certificate have been lost and the office where registration took place is not known, applications should be made to the Public Search Room★ in London.

A priority service is available which enables certificates to be despatched the next working day following receipt of order. The charge in this case is £27.50, or, when full details are known, £24.50 if ordered by post, phone or fax, and £23 if ordered online.

With any postal application, a stamped, addressed envelope should be sent, together with a cheque or postal order for the necessary amount. Applications by phone or online may be paid for by credit or debit card. When applying in person for a copy of a certificate, payment must be made at the time of application.

Scotland and Northern Ireland

For Scotland, please see Chapter 4. In Northern Ireland, contact the Registrar General (Northern Ireland)★. The charge for a standard death certificate is £10, with additional copies each costing £5. Certificates may be ordered by post, phone or online and will be supplied within three working days. There is an express service to obtain certificates within one hour; the charge for this is £25 and £10 for copies of the same certificate supplied at a later date, or £5 if full details are known and quoted. This service is not available online. Those wishing to pay by credit card should telephone the special credit-card line★.

Chapter 6

The coroner

The office of the coroner is ancient: it originated in Saxon times and received a new emphasis under the Norman regime, when the king wanted money to pursue his holy wars. The full title was *Coronæ Curia Regis* (Keeper of the Royal Pleas) and the coroner was responsible for investigating accidents such as shipwrecks – mainly to see what money could be gained for the Crown thereby – and the evaluation of treasure trove. He became responsible for keeping a record of all sudden, unexpected deaths – currently, the subject of most of the coroner's work.

The modern coroner is a qualified doctor or solicitor who is paid by the local authority, but remains independent of both local and central government, being responsible only to the Crown. He or she is assisted by the coroner's officer, usually a police officer; it is the coroner's officer who is generally in contact with the public.

The government's Review of Death Certification and Coroner Services was set up in July 2001 and its report was published in June 2003. The report recommends a number of changes to improve efficiency and increase public confidence in the process of death certification and the coroner service. None of these has been implemented at the time this book went to press.

Deaths to be reported to the coroner

When a death occurs which may not be due to natural causes, it must be reported to the coroner. Even if it is fairly evident that death was due to natural causes, but the deceased had not been seen by a doctor for 14 days prior to death, or had not been seen at all by a doctor before or after death, the coroner must be informed. In Northern Ireland the relevant period is 28 days. The coroner will then consult with the deceased's GP, who will usually be able to advise whether he or she is satisfied as to the cause of death. If the GP is satisfied that death is due to natural causes, the coroner will cease to be involved, but will send the necessary documentation to the registrar; the family will then not receive a medical certificate of the cause of death, but will be able to register the death as normal. The doctor is not legally allowed to sign the medical certificate of the cause of death if he or she has not seen the patient within 14 days, even if he or she is confident that death is due to natural causes.

In any case where the doctor is at all uncertain as to the cause of death, the death must be reported to the coroner. Any death attributable to industrial disease, or where compensation has been claimed because of this, must be reported to the coroner; in some cases, death caused or accelerated by injury received during military service, however long ago, must also be reported.

Other circumstances in which a death must be reported to the coroner include those when death:

- was sudden and unexplained
- occurred in suspicious circumstances
- was caused directly or indirectly by any kind of accident
- might have been due to neglect, any kind of poisoning, dependence on or abuse of drugs, or abortion
- was by suicide
- occurred while in prison or in police custody
- took place during a surgical operation or before recovery from the effects of anaesthesia.

Reporting the death

Anyone who is uneasy about the apparent cause of a death has the right to inform the coroner for the district. By telephoning a police station, you can find out who the relevant coroner is and how to get in touch with him or her. Or you can give information to any local police station, which will pass the information to the coroner's officer.

The information does not have to be an allegation of some crime. There may be some circumstances which you feel are contributory to the death but may not have been known to the doctor – such as an old war wound or injury – which can be established by a post mortem examination. If you believe that the deceased may have died from some industrial disease, it is obviously best to inform the coroner before the person is cremated, otherwise the matter can never be resolved.

Generally, however, it is the doctor who reports a death to the coroner, or to the police. Medical certificates of the cause of death carry a list of the type of cases that the doctor should report to the coroner. If the death comes within any of these categories, the usual practice is for the doctor to inform the coroner directly, before anyone has gone to register the death.

It may be that the registrar, when he or she gets the doctor's medical certificate of the cause of death, decides that because of the cause or circumstances of the death, he or she must report the death to the coroner. In such cases, there will be a delay before the death can be registered, which may interfere with the arrangements that the family had hoped to make for the funeral.

The coroner may decide that there is no need for further investigation, being satisfied that the cause of death is known to be natural, and that the death can be registered from the certificate provided by the doctor. In this case, the coroner sends a formal notice of the decision to the registrar of the district, and the death can then be registered in the usual way by the qualified informant. The chart on page 50 summarises all stages of the process.

If the registrar knows who the next of kin are, he or she gets in touch with them and tells them that he or she is now in a position to register the death. If the death had been reported to the coroner direct and the registrar does not know who the next of kin are, they will have to find out from the coroner's office when to go to the registrar.

Coroner's investigations

When a death is reported to the coroner and he or she decides to investigate, that death cannot be registered until the coroner provides a certificate when inquiries are complete. He or she will usually order a post mortem, which will often show that death was due to natural causes; in this case, he or she will notify the family and the registrar through the coroner's officer, and the death can then be registered in the normal way. If the funeral is to involve burial, the registrar will issue a certificate for burial. If it is to involve cremation, it is the coroner who will issue a coroner's **Form E** for cremation; one part (pink) will be given to the family or sent direct to the registrar, while the other part (yellow) will be sent to the funeral director, or direct to the crematorium.

The actual funeral will have to wait for the outcome of the coroner's investigations, but in many cases the coroner's officer will be able to give a reasonably accurate indication of how long these will take. The funeral director involved will normally consult with the coroner's officer, and will be able to make tentative funeral arrangements while the investigation is proceeding: it is not necessary to wait until the investigation ends before beginning to make arrangements.

In many cases, the coroner's involvement is a formality, and reporting a death to the coroner does not inevitably mean a post mortem or an inquest. The coroner concerned will decide what action must be taken.

Post mortem

About 125,000 post mortem examinations are carried out by order of the coroner each year, almost all to establish the cause of death. This may be to show that the death was due to natural causes, or it may be to resolve a dispute where the family believes that the death was caused by an industrial disease (a person may have suffered from an industrial illness for a considerable time but eventually die from some other, unrelated, cause). In a few cases, the post mortem provides valuable evidence of the manner of a criminal death.

The coroner orders a post mortem if the law requires this. The family of the deceased do not have to be asked to give their consent, as they would be when a hospital wants to perform a post mortem examination (see pages 22–3). The coroner arranges and pays for the post mortem.

If members of the family object to a post mortem examination for religious or other reasons, or if they have any reason to believe that the examination is not necessary, they should inform the coroner. If the coroner is still of the opinion that the examination is required, the family can apply to the High Court to reverse the decision of the coroner. This will delay arrangements for the disposal of the body.

If the post mortem reveals that the death was due to natural causes and no other circumstance warrants further investigation, the coroner notifies the registrar and the death can be registered in the usual way. In some districts, the coroner's officer or another police officer calls on the family to tell them; otherwise, the next of kin should enquire at the coroner's office every few days to find out when the coroner's notification is being sent to the registrar. The coroner has no duty to inform the next of kin of the result of the post mortem.

After the post mortem, the body again becomes the responsibility of the family. To avoid unnecessary delays, the family can arrange for a funeral director to collect the necessary forms from the coroner's office as soon as these are available and make arrangements for the funeral at the earliest suitable date.

If an inquest is required

The coroner is obliged to hold an inquest into every violent and unnatural death that is reported, and also following the death of a person in prison.

An inquest is an enquiry to determine who the deceased person was, and how, when and where that person died, and to establish the particulars that are required for the registration of the death.

An inquest is held formally and is open to the public. A person wishing to attend, but who has not been given notice of the inquest, can ask at a local police station or telephone the coroner's office to find out when the inquest is being held. The coroner may have asked for further investigations and tests to be carried out, and the date for the inquest will not be arranged until all these are complete.

Adjournment of an inquest

Coroners are increasingly prepared to open an inquest and then adjourn it 'to a date to be fixed' or for a specific number of days. While police time is not always instantly available, this enables routine enquiries to be completed without holding up burial or cremation arrangements. If it is clear to the coroner that disposal of the body will not prejudice such enquiries, he or she can take evidence of identification and of the cause of death and may then adjourn the inquest, often for a short period, until enquiries are complete – issuing the necessary order for burial or the cremation certificate before the inquest.

Adjournments also have to be made to allow extra time in more complex matters – to await the result, for example, of an inquiry into an air crash or other disaster. The coroner may provide any properly introduced person with an interim certificate of the fact of death. This will allow insurance or other payments to be claimed and the estate to be administered.

An inquest must be adjourned where a person has been charged with causing the death or with an offence connected with it that will be the subject of a trial before a crown court jury. The coroner will then send notification to the registrar for the registration of the death.

At the court

The coroner's court is a court of law with power to summon witnesses and jurors, and with power to deal with any contempt in the face of the court.

The law requires that any person with evidence to give concerning the death should attend an inquest. In practice, the coroner will have read any written statements that have been made, and will know the names of those who have been interviewed by the police and by the coroner's officers. The witnesses the coroner knows will be needed are summoned to the inquest. The summons is often an informal telephone call but there may be a written summons or a subpoena (if the witness is outside the jurisdiction of the coroner). A witness is entitled to travel expenses and to a fixed sum to compensate for loss of earnings.

If any witnesses know that they cannot attend, they should inform the coroner's office at once. When a witness has been formally summoned, there are penalties for failing to attend. Non-attendance causes inconvenience, and expense, to the family if the inquest has to be adjourned.

Unlike a trial, there are no 'sides' at an inquest. Anyone who is regarded as having a 'proper interest' may ask witnesses questions at an inquest and may be legally represented. The list of people with a proper interest includes parents, children and the spouse of the deceased, insurers and beneficiaries of an insurance policy on the life of the deceased, any person whose conduct is called into question regarding the cause of death and, in appropriate cases, a chief officer of the police, a government inspector or a trade union official.

There is a minimum amount of pomp and ceremony at an inquest. The coroner calls witnesses in turn from the main part of the court to come up to the witness box. Each witness swears or affirms to 'speak the truth, the whole truth and nothing but the truth'.

First, the coroner questions the witness; then, with his or her permission, the witness can be examined by anyone present who has a proper interest in the case (or by that person's legal representative). If you know that you will want to give evidence or examine a witness, tell the coroner's officer beforehand, so that the coroner can call you at the right moment. When all the witnesses have been heard, the coroner sums up (there are no speeches by the lawyers) and gives the verdict.

With a jury

Some inquests have to be heard before a jury. The jury is summoned in the same way as a crown court jury. In cases of industrial accidents or other incidents that must be reported to a government department, after a death in prison or in police custody or caused by the act of a police officer, and where death was in circumstances that present a danger to the public, there is always a jury.

The jury for an inquest consists of not fewer than seven and not more than 11 men or women eligible for jury service. There is no power to challenge jurors, as there is no accused person to exercise the power. The jurors are on oath. Jurors need not view the body unless the coroner directs them to.

At the conclusion of his or her enquiries, the coroner sums up the evidence to the jury and explains the law. All the findings of the inquest are then made by the jury. Jurors do not usually leave the court to discuss their decision, but they may do so. They can return a majority verdict.

The verdict

The purpose of an inquest is not only to find out who the deceased person was and how, when and where he or she came by his or her death, but also to decide the category of death. This is colloquially called the verdict, but the correct description is the conclusion. It can range from natural causes to suicide, industrial disease or misadventure. Conclusions are subject to many legal technicalities. In particular, the finding of suicide must be strictly proved: when there is no conclusive evidence of the intent to commit suicide, the coroner has to return an open verdict.

The conclusion must not appear to determine any matter of criminal liability against a named person, or any matter of civil liability.

A verdict of accidental death does not mean that there will be no prosecution in a magistrates' court or that the family cannot bring an action for damages. All it means is that it is not a case of suicide or homicide. The 'properly interested persons' are entitled to a copy of the notes of the evidence and these are often useful in subsequent proceedings.

The press and inquests

Since inquests are held in public, the press can be present. There are restrictions on the publication of the names of minors, but in other matters there are no reporting restrictions.

Death is sometimes treated as a sensational subject. Although the coroner may try to choose words carefully, people giving evidence or questioning witnesses may provide comments that can be distressing to the family. The coroner will try to ensure that the facts are as accurate as possible; the inquest may be able to dispel rumours and inaccurate assertions.

Legal advice and expenses

There should be no expense to the family arising out of an inquest. Representation by a lawyer is not necessary in the majority of inquests, and in cases where there is no controversy the family should not need to incur such expense. There is no provision for representation at an inquest under the legal aid scheme.

Many people think it wise, however, to be represented by a solicitor at the inquest in the case of death resulting from an accident or an occupational disease, because there may be compensation claims to be made later and a solicitor would be better able to make use of the evidence presented at an inquest.

Through your local Law Society* you should be able to find a solicitor who will agree to a free or small-fee interview so that a

Procedure following a death

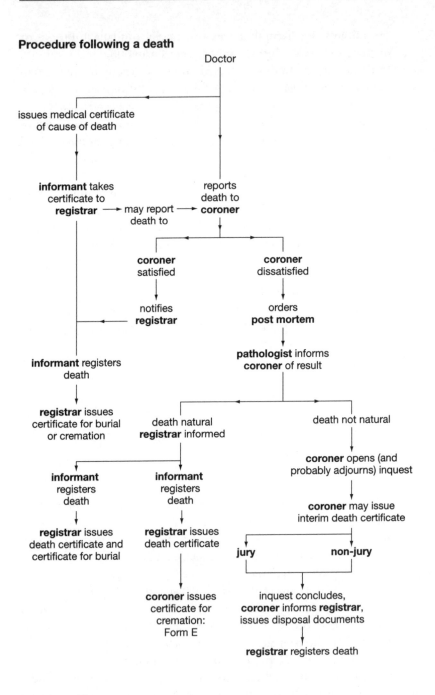

family does not pay out money unnecessarily. The solicitor may also be able to advise on the possibility of compensation.

After the inquest

In all cases other than those where someone has been charged with a serious offence, the coroner would already have sent an interim certificate for burial or cremation after adjournment of the inquest, but registration of the death usually takes place when the coroner sends a certificate after the inquest to the registrar of births and deaths of the district in which the death took place or in which the body was found. This certificate provides the registrar with the information needed to register the death (see chart on page 50). No informant is required to attend the registrar's office. The death certificates can be obtained by the family from the registrar at any time after the inquest.

INQUEST* provides information and support to people facing the inquest system after a controversial death. The organisation produces a useful pack entitled *Inquests – A Guide for Families and Friends.*

Coroner's certificate for burial or cremation

As mentioned earlier, once a death has been registered, the registrar issues a green certificate, referred to generally as the disposal certificate, authorising either burial or application for cremation. The coroner will issue the necessary documentation in certain circumstances. If the death has been reported to the coroner and a post mortem examination has been ordered, only the coroner can authorise cremation; if the body is to be buried, the registrar can issue the burial certificate. If there has been an inquest, it is the coroner who issues either an order for burial or a certificate for cremation.

No fee is charged for a coroner's order. If you lose it, you (or the funeral director) have to apply for a duplicate to the coroner who issued the original certificate.

The certificate from the coroner should be given to the funeral director. He or she will give it to the church, cemetery or crematorium officials who require it in order to bury or cremate the deceased.

Chapter 7

Organ donation for transplantation

Organ transplantation is one of the greatest medical success stories of our time. During the last 50 years it has become possible to transplant many types of body tissue, from skin to major organs. Kidney, liver, heart and heart-lung transplants have now become routine operations, and the process is constantly being refined and developed.

According to UK Transplant*, in the UK between 1 April and 31 March 2004:

- the highest number of organ transplants ever recorded – **2,867** – was carried out, thanks to the generosity of **1,244** donors
- organs from **722** people who died were used to save or dramatically improve many people's lives through **2,396** transplants
- the highest number of patients for 14 years received a kidney-only transplant, with living donation now representing one in four of all kidney-only transplants
- a further **2,365** people had their sight restored through a corneal transplant – the highest number for seven years
- a **20%** increase in non-heartbeating donation (see page 54) meant that more people than ever received a transplant from these donors
- **147** people received lung-only transplants, the highest number ever
- more than **860,000** people added their names to the NHS Organ Donor Register.

The overall effectiveness of the transplant programme is limited by the fact that the demand for organs still far exceeds their availability. Today nearly 6,000 people in the UK are waiting for an organ transplant, most for a kidney, but others for a heart, liver or lungs. However, fewer than 3,000 transplants are carried out each year.

Brain stem death

If the body of a potential donor were to be left until the traditional signs of death were apparent (lack of pulse, coldness of the body, rigor mortis and so on), the organs would have deteriorated through lack of oxygen, and would no longer be of any use.

No organ can be removed for transplantation until the patient concerned is diagnosed as being 'brain stem dead'. This occurs when the part of the brain responsible for maintaining the essential functions of the body is irreversibly damaged. This may be caused by head injury, cerebral haemorrhage, primary brain tumour, or conditions where the brain has been seriously deprived of oxygen. Such patients will normally be in hospital, with respiratory functions maintained on a ventilator. In order to determine brain stem death, specific preconditions must be met, and the cranial nerves will then be tested by a stringent set of tests laid down in the Code of Practice of the Conference of Royal Medical Colleges, revised in March 1998.

The lack of the following signs signifies irreversible damage to the brain stem:

- the pupils of the eye do not respond to light
- blinking does not occur when the cornea of the eye is touched
- there are no eye movements when the ears are irrigated with ice-cold water
- there is no gag or cough reflex
- the patient is unable to breathe unaided
- there is no response to painful stimuli
- the patient is deeply unconscious and will not wake.

If all these reflexes are found to be absent after giving the patient 100 per cent oxygen therapy, the patient's ventilator is briefly disconnected to see if he or she makes any attempt to breathe unaided. Examination is carried out by two doctors competent in this field, who have been registered for more than five years and are not members of the same transplant team. At least one must be a consultant. Two sets of tests are carried out, and if both confirm brain stem death, the legal time of death is given as the time when the first set of tests was completed.

A patient must be under 75 for his or her solid organs (heart, lung, kidneys and so on) to be suitable for transplantation; he or she must have suffered complete and irreversible brain stem damage and must normally be maintained on a ventilator. The HIV virus and CJD are contra-indications to organ donation.

In order to provide healthy organs for transplantation, the body must receive a continuous supply of oxygen, which will be artificially provided by a ventilator until the organs concerned are removed in the operating theatre by the transplant team. The donor patient will therefore appear a natural colour, the heart will continue to beat, and breathing will be maintained by the ventilator (see below). In spite of all this, the patient will be dead, totally unable to perceive or feel anything at all. Families who wish to see their relatives after organs have been removed for transplantation are normally encouraged to do so.

Heartbeating and non-heartbeating donors

Most organ donors are patients who die as a result of a severe head injury, brain haemorrhage or stroke and who are on a ventilator in a hospital intensive care unit. In these circumstances death is diagnosed by brain stem tests. These donors are called heartbeating donors. Organs such as hearts and lungs, which deteriorate very quickly without an oxygen supply, are usually donated only by a heartbeating donor.

Patients who die in hospital but are not on a ventilator can, in some circumstances, donate their kidneys, and in certain other circumstances, organs such as livers and lungs have been retrieved. Such donors are called non-heartbeating donors.

Both heartbeating and non-heartbeating donors can donate their corneas and other tissue such as skin, bone and heart valves.

Organs for transplantation

There are specific criteria for the donation of different organs, but basically the organs concerned must be in good working order. Obviously, diseased kidneys would be unsuitable, as would the lungs of a person who had smoked heavily.

The following organs are those most commonly used for transplantation.

The kidney

Each year over 2,500 patients in the UK develop chronic renal failure; kidney transplantation saves many lives, and leads to greatly improved quality of life for many more. Further, a transplant frees dialysis space (a 'kidney machine') for another patient. Kidneys are viable for up to 48 hours after retrieval from the donor; the maximum donor age is 75. The source of kidneys for transplantation is normally hospital patients maintained on ventilators following brain stem death, but under certain circumstances kidneys can be retrieved from non-heartbeating donors.

In some hospitals, patients who are certified dead on arrival or die in the Accident and Emergency department can be donors, particularly of kidneys, which are able to tolerate longer periods without oxygen than other organs.

For this to happen, however, steps have to be taken to preserve the kidneys until the next of kin are contacted. This includes a special technique in which the kidneys are flushed with a cold preservative fluid. This is done through a small tube which is inserted into a blood vessel in the groin. This must be done within minutes of death to ensure that the kidneys remain suitable for transplantation and that the deceased is not deprived of the opportunity to donate. However, organ donation itself will never take place without checking if the deceased had given consent to donate.

The liver

Liver transplants are required for patients with a congenital malformation of the liver, chronic liver disease, hepatic failure, some cases of cancer of the liver, and inborn metabolic errors. Liver transplants for people with such conditions have been successfully carried out in the UK since 1968. It is possible for a healthy liver to be split to provide transplants for two people.

The heart

The first heart transplant in the UK was carried out in 1979 at Papworth Hospital: heart transplantation is now considered for patients with severe cardiac failure who are deemed unsuitable for heart surgery and who have a decreased life expectancy.

The heart and lung

The first heart and lung transplant in the UK took place in 1985. This operation is now carried out for people with conditions leading to advanced primary lung disease, or lung disease occurring as a result of cardiac problems or cystic fibrosis.

The lungs

One or both lungs may be transplanted.

The pancreas

Transplantation of the pancreas may be used in some patients with type 1 diabetes. The pancreas may be transplanted by itself, or together with the kidneys; both are transplanted when the patient has diabetes together with renal failure. Research is in progress for islet cell transplantation.

Heart valves (tissues)

These may be transplanted following removal from a donor up to 48 hours after death. Usage is mainly for children with congenital heart defects.

The cornea (tissues)

Corneal damage is a major cause of blindness, but thousands have now had their sight restored by corneal grafting. There is no age limit for corneal donation, and the process has an excellent success rate. The need to wear spectacles does not usually affect the suitability of the donor. Corneas can be removed up to 24 hours after the heart has stopped beating; the patient does not need to be maintained on a ventilator. Corneas can be removed from patients who have died in many different circumstances; the Corneal Tissues Act allows qualified technicians to remove corneal tissue – as there are more technicians than surgeons, a greater number of donated corneas can now be retrieved.

Relatives of patients not dying in hospital who want to carry out their wishes regarding corneal donation should first of all consult the donor's GP and/or the local transplant co-ordinator. In all cases, action must be taken as quickly as possible; at any rate, within 12 hours of death. A special Corneal Transplant Service (run by the Department of Health as part of the UK transplant service, with contributory funding from the Iris Fund for the Prevention of Blindness★) takes corneas from donors to the nearest hospital grafting centre or eye bank with minimal delay.

Other transplants

Other parts of the body which can be transplanted include skin, bone, joints, connective tissue, major blood vessels, fetal cells and bone marrow.

Religious and cultural issues

Decisions to donate organs from the deceased may be complicated by religious and cultural influences. The extent and interpretation of these influences will probably vary from family to family, but the basic outline following will apply in most situations.

Buddhists do not generally object to organ donation, as helping others is a fundamental belief.

Christians: organ donation and transplantation is usually considered acceptable to Roman Catholics and most Protestants, although some Protestant sects are strongly opposed.

Christian Scientists object to all forms of organ donation and transplantation.

Hindus and **Sikhs** have no objections to organ donation, although reservations regarding post mortem operations are frequently expressed.

Jehovah's Witnesses are advised by the Watchtower Society that organ donation and acceptance for transplantation is a matter for individual choice.

Jews generally raise no objection in principle to organ donation, since the prohibitive aspect of Jewish Law can be overridden in order to save life. However, the Law insists that the success of the transplant procedure must be well established, and that no vital organs may be removed until death is confirmed by the complete cessation of all spontaneous life functions. Some Orthodox Jews object to all forms of organ donation and transplantation.

Mormons: the Church of Jesus Christ of the Latter Day Saints expresses no objection to organ donation.

Muslims are subject to Islamic Law, which states that the body must be buried as soon as possible after death. Together with reluctance to permit any interference with the dead, this tends to prohibit organ donation. However, the Muslim Law (Shariah) Council UK issued a directive in 1996 supporting organ donation and transplantation.

NHS Organ Donor Register

This register has been set up as a computer database at UK Transplant (UKT)★. The register is accessible to all transplant co-ordinators and Intensive Care Unit staff, and can be checked each time a potential donor becomes available. Anyone wishing to become a donor can contact UK Transplant via the website in the address section at the back of this book.

Relatives of donors are still asked to consent to donation, but with an individual's name included on the register and a donor card being carried, the decision is made easier for everyone. Any driving licence issued after March 1993 may be marked in the box on the back to indicate a readiness to donate organs after death, and applicants for new driving licences may indicate to the Driver and Vehicle Licensing Agency (DVLA)★ at Swansea that their wish to be entered on the NHS Organ Donor Register should be printed on the licence. Otherwise, those wishing to register may do so by post, or by using one of the special forms available from doctors, chemists, hospitals, libraries and many public places. Alternatively, they may contact the NHS Organ Donor Registration Service★. It remains very important that family and friends should be informed of an individual's wishes. Advice about how to notify the relevant people and organisations is given on pages 175–6. A leaflet entitled *Questions and Answers on the Organ Donor Register* is available free of charge from the NHS Organ Donor Register★. It answers common queries people have about organ donation. Further information may be obtained by contacting UKT.

Legal aspects of organ donation

Transplantation in Britain is governed by three items of legislation: the Human Tissues Act 1961, the Corneal Tissue Act 1986 and the Human Organs Transplants Act 1989. The first two relate to organ donation following death, while the third relates to living donors. (The above Acts will be repealed in favour of the Human Tissue Act 2004, which received Royal assent on 15 November 2004 and is expected to be implemented in 2006.)

Removal of organs can be authorised if the deceased has made a declaration in writing (usually in a will, by informing the NHS Organ Donor Register★, and/or by carrying a donor card), or an oral declaration in the presence of two witnesses that his or her organs may be so used. Alternatively, organs may be removed if, after making reasonable enquiry, there is no reason to believe that the deceased had objected to organ donation, and surviving relatives do not object. Authorisation is given by the person lawfully in possession of the body; this could be a close relative, the person owning the house where the patient died (or hospital administrator), or, in the case of a post mortem or inquest, the coroner. The law supports the view that the hospital authority is legally in possession of the body of a deceased patient until it is 'claimed'.

In any case where it is unclear whether death is due to natural causes, the coroner must be consulted in order to gain consent for organ or tissue donation. This will normally be the responsibility of the hospital consultant, and not a matter for friends or family. The coroner has the power to refuse consent to the removal of organs for transplantation if he or she feels that this may adversely affect any investigation in progress.

The practice of 'elective ventilation' (artificially ventilating a patient before death has been diagnosed solely to obtain organs later) is unlawful in the UK. For more information on organ transplant and the latest statistics visit www.uktransplant.org.uk.

ULTRA

The Unrelated Live Transplant Regulatory Authority (ULTRA)★ was set up under the Human Organ Transplants Act 1989 to approve all transplant operations involving a living donor who is not a close blood relative of the recipient. ULTRA approval is not needed for transplantation of regenerative tissues such as bone marrow.

The chairman and members of ULTRA are appointed by the Secretary of State for Health. The chairman is a doctor not involved with transplants and the members include doctors, nurses, scientists and others with a knowledge of transplant ethics. The ULTRA website gives information in several languages about ULTRA and about organ donation.

BODY

The British Organ Donor Society or BODY*, is a voluntary organisation and charitable trust formed in 1984 to help and support donor and recipient families, and to promote organ donation and transplantation.

Body donated for medical education or research

A number of people express the wish that their body should be used after death for medical research. Bodies donated in this way are used by doctors and medical students who are studying and researching the structure and function of the normal human body. (Research into specific medical diseases is not carried out in these examinations.) If such a wish was expressed by the deceased, the next of kin or executor should immediately telephone HM Inspector of Anatomy* for details of the relevant anatomy school.

Medical schools are, in fact, offered far more bodies than can possibly be accepted and it should be recognised that the offering or willing of a body to medical research does not necessarily mean that it will be accepted. Or, at the time of death there may be some specific reason why the body cannot be accepted: for instance, if the coroner is involved, if death has occurred as the result of certain illnesses, or if death occurs too far away for the relevant medical school to transport the body practically. Until acceptance of the body is confirmed, the family should continue to make arrangements for the funeral in case the body is not accepted.

Arrangements prior to death

If a body is to be accepted for medical research, it is imperative that arrangements are made with a specific medical school well before death occurs; specific forms must be completed in advance and should be left with the family, bank or solicitor along with instructions for immediate action when death occurs. If the body is accepted, arrangements will be made by the medical school for it to be collected straight away by a contracted funeral director and taken to the school. In the meantime, the next of kin or executor should obtain the medical certificate of the cause of death from the doctor in charge of the case and register the death as soon as possible. The registrar's green certificate for burial or cremation (see page 30) should also be sent to the medical school.

Donation of the brain for research

The Parkinson's Disease Society* Brain Research Centre, which is part of the Institute of Neurology at University College, London, has a unique collection of tissue donated by individuals who died either from Parkinson's disease or a related disorder. Brain donation by people with no neurological disease is also important, in order that 'control' tissue for comparison may be available. Brain tissue is used to study the effects of disease; tissue is also supplied for additional research projects throughout the UK and internationally.

Brain donation is a separate issue from other organ donation, and cannot be included on the NHS Organ Donor Register. Those indicating to the Register that all their organs may be used will not be considered for brain donation unless the Parkinson's Disease Society has been instructed to that effect. Potential donors must notify the Society of their intentions in advance, or leave clear instructions that this should be done in the event of their death.

Funeral arrangements

It is the responsibility of the medical school to arrange and pay for burial or cremation when the appropriate time comes. The family and executors need make no further arrangements: burial or cremation will be provided according to the wishes of the deceased and next of kin. If the body is eventually to be cremated, the executor may be asked to complete and sign the statutory application form for cremation, **Form A**; however, this may also be signed by the professor of the medical school.

The medical school will pay all expenses for a simple funeral, unless the relatives ask to be allowed to make their own arrangements, at which point the body will be given back and the funeral expenses will become the responsibility of the family. If the medical school makes the funeral arrangements, a simple ceremony will be conducted by a minister or priest of the faith professed by the deceased, unless otherwise requested. The medical school does not put up individual headstones.

If the relatives of the deceased do not wish to make funeral arrangements themselves, but ask for burial or cremation in some place other than that normally used by the medical school, or if they request more elaborate arrangements than those normally provided, the extra expense must be met by the family. Some medical schools give no option on the method or procedure of funerals they arrange.

Chapter 8

Decisions about the funeral

When someone dies, a number of decisions about the funeral have to be made quickly. This is often a time of considerable emotional turmoil, so great care needs to be taken to make the right decisions. Many people want to 'get the funeral over with as soon as possible'; it is wise, however, to allow enough time to recover from the shock of the first 48 hours, and plan a funeral which will be an appropriate memorial to the person who has died.

If the deceased left no specific instructions, the decision about burial or cremation is normally made by the next of kin, or the executor. Although it is usual to carry out the wishes previously expressed by the deceased, there is no legal obligation to do so. Should it prove impossible to trace either a living relative or a friend willing to act as executor, the hospital or the local authority will accept the responsibility of providing a minimum-price funeral.

Whether the funeral is to involve burial or cremation, many of the arrangements can be made by a reasonably capable individual who knows what to do. However, most people feel the need of professional help at this time, and it is still rare for a funeral to be carried out without the services of a funeral director.

Funeral directors

William Russell, the first undertaker in the UK, began business in London in 1680; he was succeeded by carpenters who specialised in producing coffins and carriage proprietors who developed special funeral carriages. These functions merged, and a profession of men who 'undertook' to provide a funeral service arose. The Victorian era saw the popularisation of elaborate, often ostentatious, and usually expensive funerals.

Undertakers are now known as funeral directors. As noted in the Foreword, the vast majority of funeral directors now belong to one of two associations: the National Association of Funeral Directors (NAFD)*, or the Society of Allied and Independent Funeral Directors (SAIF)* (since January 2004 the NAFD incorporates the former Funeral Standards Council (FSC) after its members voted to amalgamate with the NAFD).

You should be sure to choose a funeral director who is affiliated to one of the organisations listed above – if the firm is unregistered you might have no form of redress in the event of any problems. The NAFD has a Code of Practice which includes providing information about services and prices, a written estimate of charges and a detailed funeral account. Members must offer a basic funeral if requested to do so. The code covers general and professional conduct, including confidentiality and a procedure for complaints. SAIF has a similar Code of Practice and complaints procedure. Under the code, drawn up in consultation with the Office of Fair Trading (OFT), SAIF members are required to refrain from offensive or aggressive marketing techniques; this also applies to the selling of pre-paid funeral plans.

The Funeral Ombudsman Scheme is unfortunately no longer operative. However, both of the trade organisations give access to a complaints and arbitration process for those unable to resolve any problems or complaints with their local funeral director.

Funeral directors and the government

The OFT commenced an inquiry into the funerals business in March 2000, and published a report in July 2001. In preparing the report, views were invited from the funeral trade and other interested parties including burial and cremation organisations, bereavement and counselling groups, local authorities, NHS trusts, and consumer and community representatives. The number of submissions received was 188. This was complemented by a survey of 400 individuals with recent experience of arranging a funeral, and a survey of funeral directors, which produced approximately 2,000 responses.

The surveys revealed that the great majority of those arranging funerals were content, with 96 per cent of respondents saying that they were satisfied or very satisfied. The number of complaints reported to official sources was very low, and funeral directors were generally perceived to be sensitive, flexible and patient.

However, the report found that compliance with published Codes of Practice was often patchy; people were still failing to receive price lists, clear written estimates of the cost of a funeral, or details of the basic funeral service. The report stopped short of recommending new legislation for the regulation of the funeral business, but instead pushed strongly for the trade associations to seek OFT approval for robust Codes of Practice under a new initiative promoting such codes.

In February 2003 the OFT launched its consumer codes approval scheme to UK business. The code approval scheme consists of two stages.

1. The code sponsor makes a promise that its code meets the OFT's core criteria in principle. The sponsor must make sure its code contains measures designed to remove or ease consumer concerns and undesirable trading practices in its sector.
2. The code sponsor must prove that its code lives up to the initial promise. The burden of proof lies with the sponsor, who must show that the code is being effectively implemented and that consumer disputes are properly resolved.

Codes that successfully achieve the second stage will be able to carry the OFT 'approved code' logo and receive official promotion. The OFT will only approve and promote codes that are shown to safeguard and promote consumer interests beyond the basic requirements of the law.

The OFT report made a number of recommendations:

- price lists should be prominently displayed and made available for people to take away
- written estimates and invoices should be provided for all transactions
- written estimates should be given out during the initial interview, when available services are first discussed; clients should then be asked if they wish to proceed
- every funeral outlet should prominently display details of the organisation which has ultimate control of the business

- when funeral directors operate contracts for the coroner, they should not seek to influence an individual's choice of funeral director
- the funeral trade associations (the NAFD and SAIF) should seek to obtain OFT approval for Codes of Practice under the OFT's new approach to such codes
- funeral businesses which offer credit should comply with the Consumer Credit Act 1974 and the various consumer credit regulations
- literature produced by local authorities, NHS trusts, cemeteries and crematoria should be made more widely available in places that those arranging funerals are likely to visit.

The OFT, in partnership with the National Funerals College★, makes a template available to those publishing advice on funerals (particularly local authorities and NHS trusts) which sets out information for people on the practical aspects of arranging a funeral.

The OFT also encourages local directories such as *Thomson Local* and *Yellow Pages* to publish succinct guidance for people, in order to ensure that information is available prior to the making of funeral arrangements. Further information should be available in register offices, libraries, doctors' surgeries, hospitals and nursing homes.

Funeral directors and their clients

The funeral director's purpose is to assume total responsibility for organising and supplying all that is needed for a funeral, and to provide as much care as possible for the grieving relatives. Some clients want the funeral director to do everything for them, and have no wish to be directly involved in the funeral. Others want to be involved as much as possible: they may carefully think out a funeral service, select music and readings, arrange for family bearers to carry the coffin, have a member of the family give an address, and so on. It is the responsibility of the funeral director to do his or her best to carry out the client's wishes, and to assist the client with any practical participation chosen.

A small but growing number of funeral directors are now offering bereavement care services, with qualified counsellors on the staff. All should be able to refer clients to bereavement care organisations, where this is necessary. Nevertheless, the arrangement of a funeral is a business transaction and should be treated as such; it is often difficult for bereaved relatives to be businesslike in the circumstances, but most funeral directors are understanding and will give all the assistance needed. The family or friends of the deceased person should agree who is to be in charge of supervising the arrangements, and must recognise that the person who ultimately takes responsibility for the funeral arrangements is also responsible for seeing that the bill is paid. It is not part of an executor's formal duty to arrange the funeral when someone has died, although it is a responsibility often taken on.

The cost of the funeral

At the time of arranging the funeral, you should have a fairly clear idea of the kind of funeral that is wanted, and approximately how much money should be spent on it. Many people have no real idea of how much funerals are likely to cost.

Until recently, the Oddfellows Friendly Society* published an annual survey of funeral costs. They found that in 2000 (the last year for which their statistics are available) the average cost of a cremation funeral was £1,215, compared with £2,048 for a funeral including burial. There were significant regional differences with regard to burial costs – a funeral including burial cost an average of £2,646 in London, compared with an average of £1,545 in the south-west of England – but there was much less local variation in the cost of cremation funerals (the average cost of a cremation funeral in London was £1,362 compared with £959 in the north of England).

The survey also discovered that there was considerable difference between the price quoted by many funeral directors and the actual price charged when the bill arrived – sometimes a difference of over 130 per cent in London. Codes of Practice of both trade organisations require their members to provide printed price lists and written estimates in all cases.

A survey carried out in 2003 found that the Funeral Standards Council was best on this front, with over 80 per cent of those businesses surveyed offering printed price lists, compared with only 70 per cent of the National Association of Funeral Directors and the

Society of Allied Independent Funeral Directors. There is clearly room for improvement.

The funeral director can provide quotations for anything from a simple, basic funeral at minimal price to elaborate arrangements costing a great deal of money. In all cases, he or she should provide a written estimate of the cost of the proposed funeral and, when the estimate has been given, ask whether the client wishes to proceed.

Paying for the funeral in advance

While in terms of purchasing power, the cost of a funeral is less than half what it was 70 years ago, a funeral still costs a considerable amount of money. Some people who have had to pay for the funerals of relatives and friends have found it difficult to find the money to pay the bill, and have decided that they want to pay for their own funeral in advance. For some, this is not only to spare relatives from facing the cost of their funeral, but because they want to specify how things are to be done, and what they would like to take place at their own funeral. There are a number of ways in which a funeral can be paid for in advance, and these are discussed in Chapter 22.

Dealing with the costs

Some people find the expenses of a funeral very difficult to meet, and are embarrassed about telling the funeral director. In fact, one of the first things a funeral director should do is to find out whether or not there is a problem about money and, if there is, advise the client of ways in which help may be provided.

All members of both trade organisations are pledged to provide a basic funeral. This may be given a different title by different funeral directors, but it will provide:

- the removal and care of the deceased during normal office hours within a limited locality
- the arrangement of a basic funeral
- the provision of a hearse only and staff to the nearest crematorium or cemetery
- the provision of a basic coffin
- no chapel visits (although such visits are generally permitted during office hours)

- the conducting of the funeral at a time suitable to the funeral directors.

This will be provided at an inclusive package price which is significantly lower than standard charges, and many funeral directors will go well beyond the minimum requirements when supplying a basic funeral.

The funeral director will also be able to advise as to whether there is the possibility of a grant from the Social Fund (see pages 164–5). Normally, the cost of the funeral is paid for from the estate of the deceased – the money and property that has been left. Banks will normally release funds to pay for the funeral from the bank account of the deceased, if they are presented with an itemised account from the funeral director and a copy of the death certificate.

Funeral directors are in business, and will bring to the notice of clients all the various services on offer, including a range of coffins and caskets, the provision of flowers for the funeral, placing obituary notices in the local and national press, providing printed service sheets, laying on catering for family gatherings after the funeral, and providing special music such as a trumpeter, piper, or even a New Orleans Jazz band. Reputable funeral directors will bring various alternatives to your attention without attempting to get you to pay for something you do not want, but do not be pressurised into signing up for something against your better judgement.

Making the funeral arrangements

You can make preliminary arrangements with a funeral director on the telephone, but to make full arrangements for the funeral it will be necessary either for him or her to come to your home, or for you to make an appointment to visit the office. There are matters to be explained and papers to be signed: in the case of cremation, statutory documents must be signed by the client and the signature countersigned by an independent witness who is also a householder – someone not living in rented accommodation – before the funeral can take place. In practice, the funeral director making the arrangement with the client is usually acceptable as an independent witness provided he or she is a householder.

The funeral director must show you the price list for all the funerals and services he or she can provide. You can ask for this in advance, and discuss the alternatives with other members of the family or friends. If you are contacting several funeral directors, be sure you are comparing like with like: ask for printed price lists, not just verbal estimates, and be very suspicious if none is available. Members of the main trade organisations must display printed price lists at their premises (the OFT recommends outside their premises, if possible), and provide copies for people to take away on request. Find out what is included in the inclusive prices, and visit the funeral director's premises if at all possible – you can do this without any commitment.

The estimate for the funeral account will be in two parts:

- **fees that the funeral director will charge you for his or her services**: for collecting the body of the deceased; caring for the deceased person until the funeral; arranging and conducting the funeral; and supplying the hearse, limousine, staff and so on
- **fees that the funeral director will pay to third parties (disbursements)** for services supplied on your behalf: doctors' fees for cremation papers; crematorium or burial fees; and fees for the church, minister, organist, gravediggers, obituaries, flowers and so on.

The funeral director will pay for all or most of the disbursements in advance and will usually add the relevant amounts to the funeral account, to be paid after the funeral. However, an increasing number of funeral directors ask their clients to pay for disbursements in advance, usually at the time of the funeral arrangement.

Many funeral directors make no charge, or only a nominal charge, for the funerals of babies and small children; some will extend this courtesy to funerals for children up to school-leaving age. The funeral director will have little option, however, but to pass on fees or disbursements that may be charged by churches, crematoria or burial authorities.

When funeral arrangements have been made to the satisfaction of the client, he or she will often be asked to sign the arrangement form as a contractual agreement that the funeral director will supply the services specified and that the client will, according to the funeral director's terms and conditions, in due course pay for them. It should always be remembered that the person who takes responsibility for arranging the funeral also becomes responsible for ensuring that the funeral account is paid.

Burial or cremation

The choice of cremation rather than burial may involve many different factors, but as far as cost is concerned, cremation is usually cheaper – sometimes much cheaper. Charges vary around the country, but an average cost of £300 to £400 for cremation must be set against an average cost of £400 to £600 for burial of a local resident in a municipal cemetery.

Ancillary fees of £111 for doctors' cremation papers (see below) set against anything up to £300 for gravediggers' fees (when not included in the charges of the cemetery authority) weight the difference even more. Fees for burial in some country cemeteries are often considerably cheaper for local residents; fees for non-residents, where they are accepted for burial, may be doubled, and sometimes tripled or quadrupled. Burial in Church of England churchyards is usually cheaper than in a municipal or private cemetery; the fees for 2005 were £236 (£84 for the funeral service in church and £152 for the following burial in the churchyard, to which the cost of digging the grave must be added). But most churchyards have little, if any, grave space left, and can accommodate only the burial of ashes caskets in small plots, or arrange for a second interment in a double-depth grave.

The fees for the funeral services of the Church of England churches and clergy are set annually by the Archbishops' Council, and are followed by most other denominations. The fixed annual fees are divided into two parts, one part to the parochial church council (PCC), which includes the service of the church building and verger, and the other part going towards the provision of the incumbent's stipend. Extra costs for heating and use of the organ etc. will sometimes be added; these fees will be the same for burial as for cremation (see Chapter 10).

The Church of England will charge the same fee for a minister's services (£84 in 2005) if the funeral takes place at a crematorium chapel, or anywhere other than the church of which he or she is the incumbent. In central areas of large cities, burial fees may increase to many hundreds – sometimes thousands – of pounds. The growing shortage of space for burials in existing cemeteries and the difficulties incurred in providing new cemeteries inevitably mean considerable increases in costs. Many cemetery authorities do not provide the services of a gravedigger, in which case costs will be incurred as mentioned above.

It must be remembered that the cost of funerals involving cremation is not limited to the charges made by the local crematorium. Special certificates (Forms B and C) made out by two independent doctors are required, for which the British Medical Association sets a charge, normally increasing annually; the fee for each certificate in 2005 was £55.50, a total of £111.

Coffins

Some funeral directors charge for a complete service, including a coffin, while others break their costs down into charges for vehicles, professional services and so on, and charge separately for the client's choice of coffin. In the case of an inclusive service the choice of a more expensive type of coffin usually provides a more elaborate type of funeral. Different firms include different items in their inclusive charges; some charge extra for mourners' limousines, a car for the minister and for viewing the deceased during evenings or at weekends, while others would include these and other items within the basic fee. A funeral director should be able to show clients examples or illustrations of the different coffins and caskets he or she can supply.

The material from which a coffin is made greatly affects the price: the most basic type of coffin will be made from chipboard laminated with plastic foil; a standard type from wood-veneered chipboard or MDF (medium density fibreboard); and a superior coffin or casket from solid wood, such as mahogany or ash. Cardboard coffins are now readily available, and are often chosen by families who want to paint or otherwise decorate their coffin. Woven coffins made from wicker, willow or bamboo are increasing in popularity, and are often chosen by those who feel strongly about environmental issues. It is advisable to inspect these, as all coffins, before deciding on a purchase.

There is little variation in the cost of coffin linings and fittings, although if solid brass handles are requested, these will be expensive. Remember to notify the funeral director if the coffin should or should not bear a (Christian) cross. For cremation, metal fittings are inadmissible; handles and fittings are made of plastic which has been electroplated with brass or nickel. Indeed, there are rigid by-laws which control the materials used in the construction of coffins for cremation. For each cremation, the funeral director must sign that he or she has conformed to the government's and the crematorium's requirements.

Some funeral directors buy plain coffins, which are then lined and fitted with handles according to their client's choice; others offer their clients a variety of coffins already fitted and lined.

Each coffin must be fitted with a nameplate which contains the name of the deceased; it is normal for the plate also to contain the date of death and the deceased's age. It is worth remembering that the coffins offered for simple, basic funerals are intended for cremation rather than burial. In order to keep costs and prices down, the coffin is constructed to be suitable for carrying into a crematorium and placing on the catafalque but may not be sturdy enough to withstand the rigours of being lowered into a grave. It is advisable to choose a more sturdily constructed coffin if burial is envisaged; this does *not* mean buying the most expensive coffin – the funeral director will advise accordingly.

Other costs

It must be remembered that the total cost of the funeral will consist of the fees the funeral director will charge for his or her professional services, the fees paid to other agencies on behalf of the client, and any special services that are required beyond those supplied in the standard funeral package (such as the removal of a body from a house or nursing home out of standard working hours, additional limousines, and a charge for mileage if the funeral involves travelling some considerable distance). There will also be an extra charge if the body is to be taken into church on the evening before the funeral, or for supplying a casket for the burial of cremated remains (ashes).

The funeral director should give an itemised written estimate of the costs and a formal confirmation of funeral arrangements. Some people may feel that they do not want to be involved in too many practical decisions about the funeral, and want to leave it to the funeral director; it is still important for them to be given a written estimate of the cost. The estimate may well be amended as the bereaved relatives discuss the developing funeral arrangements, and decide on changes, such as the placement of obituaries, or an extra limousine, or indeed reduce the bill by removing various items from the funeral arrangement. The estimate is a clear outline of what the funeral is likely to cost, but is *not* the bill: the funeral director will submit the account shortly after the funeral takes place.

Funeral directors will explain the charges and conditions made for different churches in the local area, and the different fees charged by cemeteries and crematoria.

Nonconformist churches such as the Methodist, Baptist and United Reformed Churches do not usually set fees for funerals, but tend to accept the same fees as those laid down by the Church of England (see page 71). Fees for the funeral of a member of the church or congregation are frequently waived. Such churches do not usually have graveyards, although there are exceptions: church funeral services are usually followed by cremation, or burial in a local cemetery.

Roman Catholic churches do not set fees for funeral services either, but will accept a gift towards the ministry of the church. Sometimes this is taken care of by the family of the deceased person, but more usually the funeral director will provide a gift commensurate with the fees paid to the Church of England.

Generally, the cost of a funeral, including cremation, is unlikely to come to less than £1,200: the average cost of a cremation funeral was £1,215 in 2000. The cost of a funeral including burial is likely to be considerably more, and is seldom less than £1,800: the average cost for a funeral with burial in 2000 was £2,048. Currently, burial funeral costs are rising by about 12.5 per cent each year, and cremation funeral costs by about 6 per cent. The cost of burials (not the whole funeral) rose by 130 per cent between 1991 and 2000, compared with a rise of 67 per cent for cremation costs during the same period.

Price levels, especially for burials, vary enormously between different parts of the country, especially in London and other large cities. Prices also vary between local funeral directors. If you are checking on the different prices for services charged by local funeral directors, it is advisable to visit the offices, ask for a price list and inspect the premises; you will gain a far better idea of the services available than by making a telephone call. Not only may the prices charged vary considerably, but so may the quality and condition of vehicles, chapels of rest and so on. No funeral director should object to showing you what he or she can provide, and the Codes of Practice of both trade organisations require funeral directors to provide you with a printed price list to take away.

Help with funeral costs

Anyone on a low income who has great difficulty in meeting funeral costs may be able to obtain help from the Social Fund, but there are rigid criteria for gaining such assistance. The applicant or their partner must be receiving one or more of the following: Income Support, income-based Jobseeker's Allowance, Pension Credit, Council Tax Benefit, Housing Benefit, Child Tax Credit (at a higher rate than the family element), or Working Tax Credit (where a disabled worker is included in the assessment). For more information see pages 163–4.

A number of local authorities now provide a municipal funeral service. This is done by contracting with local funeral directors for the provision of simple, low-cost funerals for residents of the local authority area. The London boroughs of Lambeth and Lewisham operate such a scheme, and a similar one exists in Cardiff. The cost is considerably less than that of an average local funeral.

Relatives of a member of the armed forces who dies in service may receive help with funeral costs from the Ministry of Defence (see Chapter 17).

When someone without relatives dies, and no one can be found to pay for the funeral, the local district council where the person died (or hospital, if the death occurred in hospital) is responsible for arranging the funeral and paying for the cost. If the police have a body in their charge for which no relative can be traced, they notify the local authority which will then provide a minimum-price funeral. Many hospitals have a 'funeral fund' and most local authorities have contracts with local funeral directors for the provision of such funerals. Arrangements vary considerably in different areas. If the provision of such a funeral is likely to be needed, acquaintances of the deceased must not approach any funeral director to begin making funeral arrangements. If they do, responsibility for funeral costs will then fall upon them, as local authorities have no power to reimburse costs where a third party has already made funeral arrangements. The local authority may recoup the cost of the funeral from the estate of the deceased, or from anyone who was responsible for maintaining the deceased while still alive.

Most funeral directors are sympathetic to clients with little money who have to arrange a funeral but do not meet the criteria for a grant from the Social Fund. The majority will provide a basic funeral at minimum cost; it is sometimes possible to spread this cost over a number of monthly payments. The funeral director should be told at the outset if there are financial difficulties, and ways will usually be found to give practical assistance.

Chapter 9

Cremation

At the time of writing more than 70 per cent of funerals involve cremation. The high proportion of cremations is due not only to the fact that cremation is almost always cheaper than burial (the average cost of a burial was over £800 more than the average cost of a cremation in 2000), but also to a radical shift in attitudes that has developed since cremation began to be popular in the early years of the last century.

There are about 240 crematoria in the UK, most of which are operated by municipal authorities, although private companies own a small proportion. Each crematorium has its own scale of fees, which usually increase annually; there is considerable variation in fees, but nothing like the great disparity which occurs in burial fees. Most crematoria publish brochures giving details of their services and fees, and most organise open days, usually on a Sunday, when the general public can investigate the whole cremation procedure. Most crematoria are open during office hours from Monday to Friday, although some open on a Saturday morning. A number will offer cremation outside normal working hours at an extra charge, which is usually quite considerable. Almost all will have a 'garden of remembrance', landscaped grounds in which the cremated remains (ashes) of the deceased can be scattered or buried following a cremation funeral.

When the government brought in the Environmental Protection Act in 1990, many crematoria had to install new, more efficient cremators in order to conform with the regulations regarding pollution and the environment. This has been an enormously expensive operation, and the charges set by most crematoria have risen considerably in recent years as a result.

Further regulation regarding the removal of mercury emissions from crematoria is likely within the next few years; this is likely to raise the cost of each cremation by as much as £70.

The formalities

Before cremation can take place, the cause of death has to be established beyond any reasonable doubt. Should any question arise concerning the cause of death after a burial, an exhumation and pathological examination can take place; this is obviously not possible following a cremation. If the deceased's doctor knows the cause of death beyond any reasonable doubt, he or she will sign the medical certificate of the cause of death, which, when given to the next of kin, will enable the death to be registered.

If the funeral is to involve cremation, the doctor must also carry out an examination and complete a certificate of examination (**Form B**), which must be corroborated by a second doctor on a similar form (**Form C**). The second doctor must be independent of the first, and both must be of not less than five years' standing. A fee, set annually by the British Medical Association, will be charged for each form completed: the fee was £55.50 for each form in 2005. This procedure may well change when the recommendations of the Review of Death Certification and Coroner Services and the Shipman Report are decided upon and implemented.

If someone dies in hospital, the forms will be completed by the doctor who treated the patient and another doctor at the same hospital who is not of the same ward and has not less than five years' standing. The same fees will be payable.

If the doctor treating the deceased person is in any way unsure of the cause of death, the coroner must be informed. A post mortem will normally follow, and if death is found to be due to natural causes, there will be no inquest and the coroner will provide a coroner's **Form E** for cremation (or, where relevant, a coroner's order for burial). Where the coroner is thus involved, **Forms B** and **C** will not be required, and no fees will be charged.

Unlike burial, which can sometimes take place on the authority of a disposal certificate issued before registration, cremation cannot take place until the correct documentation has been produced and the death registered.

Documents required for cremation

When death is due to natural causes and the coroner is not involved, four additional statutory forms have to be completed before cremation can take place. The first form must be completed by the next of kin or the executor, and the others by three different doctors. These forms are issued by the local crematorium; funeral directors keep a supply, and doctors usually keep a supply of those relevant to them.

The forms required are:

- medical certificate of the cause of death (issued by the deceased's doctor to the next of kin)
- registrar's certificate for burial or cremation (the green certificate issued by the registrar following registration)
- **Form A** (the application for cremation)
- Form to authorise the disposal of the cremated remains (ashes): usually reverse of **Form A**
- service details form (gives the crematorium details of the funeral service to take place)
- **Form B** (signed by the deceased's GP or hospital consultant)
- **Form C** (signed by an independent doctor)
- **Form F** (signed by the local medical referee after scrutiny of **Forms B** and **C**).

Form A is the application for cremation, and has to be completed by the next of kin or the executor, and countersigned by a householder who knows him or her personally. In most situations, the funeral director will be acceptable as counter-signatory, but some crematoria insist on someone else signing the form.

Forms B and **C** are on the same piece of paper, which also often includes **Form F**. **Form B** has to be completed by the doctor who attended the deceased during the last illness; he or she must examine the body before the form can be completed. This may or may not be the patient's normal GP. The doctor may have to ask the relatives or acquaintances for some of the information the forms require: for instance, whether the deceased had undergone any operation during the final illness, or within a year before death, whether the deceased had been fitted with a pacemaker, and whether or not it had been removed (pacemakers must be removed before cremation to avoid an explosion).

Form C is the confirmatory medical certificate, and must be completed by a doctor who has been registered as a medical practitioner in the UK for five years or more. He or she must not be a relative of the deceased, nor a relative or partner of the doctor who completed **Form B**. If two hospital doctors complete **Forms B** and **C**, they must not have worked on the same ward, attending the same patient. The second doctor also has to see the body before completing the form.

Form F, the fourth statutory document, has to be signed by the medical referee of the crematorium, stating that he or she is satisfied with the details on **Forms B** and **C**, or the coroner's certificate for the cremation. The medical referee has the authority to prevent cremation taking place and may query details given in the forms supplied. If it is felt necessary, he or she may order a post mortem to take place, or refer the matter to the coroner, if this has not already been done. The relatives of the deceased have no right to prevent this post mortem; if they do not wish it to take place, then they must forgo cremation and opt for burial instead. If they do agree to the post mortem, it is quite likely that they will have to pay for it. Cases such as this are extremely unusual, however: the funeral director and crematoria staff will usually notice any anomalies before it reaches the stage of submission to the medical referee. Most crematoria include the fee for the services of the medical referee in the total charge for cremation.

When the coroner is involved and has ordered a post mortem, he or she will issue a certificate for cremation for which there is no charge; in this case, **Forms B** and **C** are not required. When a death is reported to the coroner, he or she must be informed at the outset if the funeral is to involve cremation, so that the appropriate certificate may be issued. This is statutory **Form E**, and (if there is to be no inquest) it will be supplied as a pink form to the relatives so that they may register the death, and as a yellow form to the funeral director for submission to the crematorium. Sometimes the appropriate forms may be sent by the coroner direct to the registrar and crematorium.

In very rare cases where the coroner has a reason for not allowing cremation to take place, he or she will issue a coroner's order for burial only. The coroner may be able to inform the relatives that cremation may be possible at a later date, when the investigations

Documents for cremation

Document	Source	Function	Recipient
registrar's certificate for burial or cremation (green certificate) *or*	registrar	required before funeral can take place	via relative and funeral director to crematorium authorities; Part C returns to registrar
coroner's certificate for cremation: Form E	coroner after post mortem or inquest	replaces Form B/C	
Form A	funeral director or crematorium: to be completed by executor or next of kin	applies for cremation and confirms arrangements	crematorium
Form B*	doctor or hospital	certifies cause of death	medical referee at crematorium
Form C*†	doctor or hospital, to be completed by second doctor	confirms cause of death	medical referee at crematorium
ashes disposal form	funeral director or crematorium	confirms arrangements, gives instructions for disposal of ashes	crematorium authorities
Form F	medical referee	confirms information in Forms B & C or E	crematorium authorities
certificate for disposal of cremated remains	crematorium	confirms date and place of cremation	via relatives to burial authorities
certificate of cremation	crematorium	copy of entry in register	executor or next of kin

*Forms B and C are not required if the coroner is involved and issues Form E.
†Form C is not required if a hospital post mortem is conducted by a doctor qualified for more than five years.

have been completed; the relatives in this case must be prepared to wait for cremation at a later date, or opt for burial.

If the body of a stillborn child is to be cremated, a special medical certificate has to be completed by a doctor who was present at the birth, or who examined the body after birth. No second medical certificate is required, but the medical referee still has to complete **Form F** (see page 80).

The table on page 81 summarises the function of each form.

Fees

Fees for a cremation funeral include the charges made by the crematorium (which usually include the fee for the medical referee, who has to sign **Form F** before the cremation can take place), the fees for the doctors' certificates and, normally, a standard fee for the minister who takes the service. Sometimes the organist's fee is included in a charge levied by the crematorium, although at other times he or she is engaged separately and charges a separate fee. All these are normally paid in advance by the funeral director, and added to the final funeral account.

The fees charged by crematoria vary from one district to another, but are generally in the region of £300–£400 (2005), with additional fees sometimes charged for those deceased persons who did not live in the local district. Unlike burial fees, these are not usually doubled, but involve only a relatively small extra charge. Many crematoria have now abandoned this practice, and apply the same charges to all, regardless of where they lived.

The doctors who prepare and sign **Forms B** and **C** are each entitled to a fee of £55.50 (2005). Should a doctor be required to remove a cardiac pacemaker (which is essential if cremation is to take place), a fee for this will be a matter for negotiation between the doctor and the local Primary Care Trust. This removal, however, may be carried out by the funeral director's staff as part of his or her inclusive charges. Doctors are also entitled to charge travelling expenses of 56.4p per mile when signing forms for cremation. This charge for expenses normally increases annually.

Sometimes, when death has occurred in hospital, the hospital may wish to carry out a post mortem examination to improve understanding of the patient's medical condition. This is not mandatory, and the consent of the relatives must be obtained; if given, **Form C** will not be required, providing that the post mortem is carried out by a pathologist of not less than five years' standing and the result known by the doctor who signed Form B. Hence only one fee of £55.50 (2005) will be charged. In certain cases, the post mortem examination may be carried out by a pathologist of less than five years' standing; in this event another doctor who does have five years' standing must confirm the results and complete **Form C** and the full £111 will be charged.

Before a hospital (or consented) post mortem takes place, under new rules pathologists are required to gain details of consent from the next of kin, and to give clear information about any part of the body which may have been removed, and explain why. New guidelines issued by the Royal College of Pathologists also make clear that, unless agreement has been reached about the long-term retention of organs or tissue for research and teaching, hospitals must ascertain whether relatives wish these materials to be returned to the family so that they can make their own arrangements for disposal, or whether they are willing for the hospital to do so. The College also recommends improved training for doctors seeking consent for post mortems, suggests that the difference between removing tissue samples or whole organs be explained to relatives, and advises that they be informed about any organs which are kept. For more information on hospital post mortems, see Chapter 2.

Most crematoria charge reduced fees for the funerals of children up to school-leaving age, and waive charges for infants under one year old. Practices vary, but the fees are often in the region of 20 per cent of the full adult fees. Bereaved parents considering a cremation funeral for their babies and infants should be advised that there will very seldom be any cremated remains available for later interment.

The service

Charges for cremation usually include a fee for the use of the crematorium chapel, whether or not it is used for a religious service. The chapel is non-denominational, catering for a range of religions. Some crematoria have a rota of chaplains of various denominations, but usually arrangements for a clergyman to conduct the funeral service are made by the relatives or the funeral director. There is no law requiring a religious service at a funeral, and a small but growing number of people opt for a non-religious funeral service. The British Humanist Association* or the National Secular Society* will put you in touch with someone in your area who can conduct such services; most funeral directors will be able to refer you to someone, and some are experienced themselves at conducting such services.

Most crematoria have facilities for playing music while the congregation enters and leaves, and this may be chosen by the relatives.

Crematoria work to a strict appointments system, so services must be fairly short, unless a special booking is made for a longer period, which will cost extra. Most crematoria allow only 30 minutes between appointments, some allow 45 minutes, and a few only 20 minutes.

Memorials

Most crematoria have various forms of memorial. There is usually a 'Book of Remembrance' in which the name of the deceased may be suitably inscribed; other memorials involve small stone wall-plaques, memorial rose bushes with a plaque giving the name of the deceased, or a display of spring flowers. Few now provide a columbarium, where ashes may be stored in a small niche in a special wall, but some crematoria allow ashes caskets to be buried in that part of the grounds known as the 'Garden of Remembrance', or in an adjoining cemetery.

All of these will involve special charges, and are usually offered to the bereaved a couple of weeks after the funeral. Do not allow yourself to be pressurised into buying a memorial that is not something you really want. Take time to consider all the options and costs, and discuss the matter thoroughly with all involved. You may decide that you do not want any form of memorial.

Some new or recently refurbished crematoria provide extensive means of memorial in carefully landscaped grounds. Some have made new provision for the storage or burial of ashes caskets, and one or two have created elaborate water gardens with provision for personal memorials to be set in place.

Cremated remains

The cremated remains or ashes of the deceased may be scattered in the grounds of the crematorium where the funeral took place, taken away to be scattered elsewhere, kept by the family, or buried in a local churchyard or cemetery after making the necessary arrangements. The ashes may also be buried in private ground without obtaining permission from any authority, but it should be remembered that the law treats the burial of cremated remains in the same way as full burials, and to remove them without a licence from the Home Office is a criminal offence.

The crematorium will not normally charge a fee for scattering ashes shortly after a funeral, but a fee will be incurred if the ashes are stored and scattering takes place at a later date. There will also be a fee of about £25 if the ashes are to be scattered in the grounds of a crematorium different from the one where the funeral took place. The Church of England fee for the burial of ashes in a churchyard is £76 (2005), or £30 if buried in a local cemetery – to which the fees of the cemetery authority must be added. Fees for the interment of ashes in municipal or private cemeteries vary greatly. Some crematoria are reluctant to arrange the transport of ashes from one locality to another. The funeral director will be able to arrange this, or relatives can make their own arrangements with a national courier for a fee of £20 to £30 within the UK mainland.

Since 1999, considerable publicity has been given to the matter of the dignified disposal of human organs removed for medical research during post mortem examinations, especially in relation to babies and small children. Until recently, relatives of such children experienced considerable distress following the revelation of such retention, and additional concern when they discovered that it was not legal for crematoria to cremate these organs separately after the funeral had taken place. In February 2000 the law was changed to allow crematoria to participate in such procedures. Those concerned should consult their local crematorium superintendent, who will be able to give advice.

A leaflet entitled *What You Should Know About Cremation* provides information about frequently asked questions, and is available from the Cremation Society of Great Britain★.

Chapter 10

Burial

Despite the fact that fewer than 30 per cent of bereaved relatives choose to have their loved ones buried rather than cremated, those who take this option face increasing difficulties in finding a churchyard or cemetery where the burial can take place. Most of the 1,124 traditional cemeteries in the UK are almost full.

Most cemeteries are municipally operated by either district, parish or borough councils, with private companies owning only a small proportion. The Church of England owns many more burial grounds in the form of churchyards, but most of these are full or disused, with space available only for the burial of small ashes caskets. Many local authorities, especially those in urban areas, experience considerable difficulty finding ground available for new cemeteries; the growing requirements of land for building new homes, together with the objections of those living close to the proposed development, greatly restrict the availability of burial space.

However, increasing interest in 'green' funerals has seen the emergence of over 180 woodland burial grounds in the last few years. These are not necessarily cheaper than traditional cemeteries, but this practice is set to become one of the major contributory factors in making new burial ground available. Interest in burial on private land is also increasing.

Burial in cemeteries

When someone dies and the family decides that the funeral shall involve burial, arrangements for the funeral can be made very quickly. However, the date and time of the funeral should not be confirmed until the death has been registered, and the registrar's certificate for burial or cremation (or the coroner's order for burial, should he or she be thus involved) has been obtained. This must be given to the funeral director for onward transmission to the burial authority, or, if a funeral director is not involved, taken directly to the cemetery office. Without this documentation, the funeral cannot proceed.

Most cemeteries are non-denominational, but a few are owned by a particular religious denomination; burial in such places is usually restricted to members of that denomination. Some cemeteries have a section of the ground consecrated by dignitaries of the Church of England, but the opening of new burial grounds is often attended by a service of consecration for the whole of the area. Some cemeteries have ground dedicated to, or reserved for, other specific religious groups, together with a separate section of general ground. In most cemeteries, any type of religious service can be held, or none at all.

Most older cemeteries have a chapel in the grounds which is non-denominational, and can be used for funeral services when a service in the church is not desired. However, many of these chapels are seldom used: a considerable number have neither lighting nor heating, and some buildings may be damp and dilapidated.

Some cemeteries provide the services of a chaplain for burial services on a rota basis; where this happens there is usually a choice of Roman Catholic, Church of England or Free Church chaplains.

Graves

Although people often refer to purchasing a grave plot, in reality this is seldom possible. Grave plots are usually 'leased', with the cemetery authority retaining the rights of ownership. A grave plot may be leased by purchasing the exclusive right of burial in that plot for a specific period not exceeding 100 years. Often the period is less, for example 75 or 50 years.

There is a charge for purchasing this exclusive right of burial, at prices which vary enormously across the country. The fee charged does not usually include the automatic right to bury someone in the plot; for this, a further interment fee will be charged. Thus the cost of burial will usually consist of the fee for purchasing the exclusive right of burial in a particular plot of land, plus the interment fee when the funeral takes place; the cost of digging the grave may be included in this charge, or may be added to it if a gravedigger has to be employed separately. Purchase of the exclusive right of burial also bestows the right to put a memorial in place, but a further fee will be charged and restrictions are often placed on the type of memorial permitted.

For this type of private grave, a deed of grant is issued, sometimes referred to as a certificate of ownership, for which some cemeteries make a charge. The deed should be kept somewhere safe, and the family or executors should know where it is. It may have to be produced in evidence before the grave can be opened for an interment, and the signature of the owner of the deed obtained before the burial can take place. If the owner of the deed has died, the cemetery authority will probably require some alternative disclaimer if the deed has not been re-registered. After the funeral, the deed will be endorsed with details of the burial and returned to the executors.

It is not essential to purchase the exclusive right of burial; indeed, some cemeteries will not permit their clients to do so. Application can be made to the burial authority for interment in what is often called a 'common grave': in this case the burial authority reserves the right to bury another person in the same plot, usually with certain restrictions. It may be possible in these situations to put up a small memorial or plaque, but often this is not allowed. In some cemeteries, no interments will take place in such a grave for a set number of years – usually 7 or 14 – after the first burial, except to bury another member of the same family. Most graves are dug deep enough to allow two or three burials (sometimes more) to take place.

Sometimes people are aware that a family grave exists in a certain cemetery or churchyard – sometimes the knowledge is limited to a certain town – and they experience considerable difficulty in tracing its exact location. Online UK cemetery databases which can help people with their searches have begun to spring up, with examples in London, Coventry, Hertfordshire, Bristol and York; the number of such databases is likely to increase as popularity grows. One such example is *www.birmingham.gov.uk/cemeteries*. The Commonwealth War Graves Commission★ also offers a search facility. On a less serious note, the US website *www.findagrave.com* will help you to find the grave of your favourite celebrity.

In the past, cemeteries offered a wide choice of types of grave, with a variety of memorials. Mausoleums or 'brick' graves with a bricked (or concrete) floor and brick-built walls could be constructed. In the few places where such graves are still available, the formalities and construction can take weeks, and are always very expensive. The funeral will thus take longer to arrange, and higher interment fees may be required in addition to the cost of the grave. A lawn grave, which consists of a headstone with mown grass over and between the grave areas, is now the only option available in most cemeteries; kerbs, surrounds and elaborate memorials are not permitted.

The cost of maintaining cemeteries has soared, and most modern burial authorities want to make maintenance economic and as easy as possible. Families planning a funeral which involves burial in a local cemetery should make enquiries about memorials as soon as possible, as considerable distress can be caused if an elaborate memorial is planned and restrictions are only discovered after the burial has taken place.

Burial fees in cemeteries

Fees for burial in a cemetery vary widely even within the same locality. They are set by the owners, under the terms of the appropriate Acts of Parliament. Fees and regulations are usually displayed at the cemetery. If you telephone or write to the superintendents of local cemeteries, you will be sent lists or brochures, from which you will be able to compare charges and conditions. A cemetery's fee may include the services of an officiant (there may be a rota of Anglican, Catholic and Free Church ministers) and a gravedigger; most will expect the funeral director or person taking responsibility for the funeral to arrange for these services on their own behalf. Some cemeteries do not allow flowers to be planted or put on graves; many forbid artificial flowers. Regulations regarding memorials may be very restrictive, and if a memorial is planned, the rules must be scrutinised very carefully.

In most local authority cemeteries, a higher fee is required for those who are not residents within the local council district; these are usually double the normal fees, but may be treble, or even more.

There may be some concessions for former residents and their relatives. Interment fees are less for children than for adults; each cemetery authority fixes its own fees and defines its own age limits.

Most local authority cemeteries have an application form which must be completed and signed by the next of kin or executor. All fees have to be paid in advance, and the fee and necessary documents sent to the cemetery office by a stipulated date before the funeral. If a funeral director is involved, he or she will deal with this, and add the fees to the funeral account. The funeral director may request the payment of such disbursements in advance, or be prepared to wait for repayment of the fees on presentation of the account after the funeral has taken place.

A fee will be charged for the placement of a memorial, and a further fee charged by the cemetery if a second inscription is added to the existing memorial following a second burial in the same grave. For a second or subsequent burial to take place, the existing memorial will have to be removed and replaced; the cemetery authority will not normally be involved in this and will charge no fee, but the memorial mason who carries out the work will charge for its removal and replacement, normally two separate fees. Funeral directors will generally deal with these charges, adding them to the funeral account as above.

Burial in churchyards

Anyone, whether Christian or not, whose permanent address is within the ecclesiastical parish, is in theory entitled to be buried in the parish churchyard, even if he or she dies away from the parish. In practice, there may well be no space left in the churchyard, and this right cannot be transferred to municipal cemeteries. Many old churchyards are closed to further burials, but some churches have arranged to have extended burial grounds separate from the church, where parishioners have the right of burial. Ex-parishioners and non-parishioners with family graves, or those whose close relatives have been buried in the churchyard, have the right of burial there, as does anyone who dies in the parish.

It is the incumbent (vicar, rector or priest in charge) and the parochial church council (PCC) who decide whether someone

Documents for burial

Document	Source	Function	Recipient
registrar's certificate for burial (the disposal certificate) *or* if inquest is to be held: coroner's order for burial	registrar coroner	required before burial can take place authorises burial	via relative and funeral director to burial authorities; Part C returned to registrar
application for burial in cemetery	from cemetery via funeral director, usually signed by executor or next of kin	applies for burial and confirms arrangements	cemetery authorities
grave deeds *or* faculty	cemetery *or* diocese	proves right to grave	burial authorities
copy of entry in burial register	burial authorities	proves burial and locates grave	executor or next of kin

who has no right by law or custom to burial in the churchyard may be buried there, and what fee to charge. For a non-parishioner, or someone with no connection with the parish, the charges are likely to be higher than for a parishioner.

Burial fees in churchyards

For people who live within the boundaries of the local parish, certain fees are payable to the local church for funeral services in church followed by burial in the churchyard. A proportion of these fees is paid to the incumbent as a contribution towards his or her salary, and the remainder to the PCC; these fees are specified by the Archbishop's Council under the Parochial Fees Order, and usually increase annually.

The current fee payable for a funeral service in church is £84, and the fee for a subsequent burial in the churchyard is £152, making a total of £236 (2005). The same fees apply if the whole funeral takes place at the graveside in the churchyard. If the church service is followed by burial in a municipal or private cemetery, the church fee of £84 remains the same, but the interment fee (which will probably be considerably more than £152) must be paid to the local authority or owners of the cemetery. Such fees vary considerably, but no interment fee is payable to the church. Any payment for an organist, choir or bell ringers is additional; there is often a charge for heating and use of the organ, in addition to the organist's fee. Diocesan guidelines state clearly that the services of a verger should be included in the fee of £84, to be paid out of the proportion allowable to the PCC; in practice, a verger's fee of £10 to £30 will frequently be charged for funeral services held in church.

The fee for burial in a churchyard without having had a service in a church of the parish beforehand is £182; the same fee is payable if the churchyard burial does not take place immediately following the church service, but takes place on a subsequent occasion. If a graveside service is held before a churchyard burial, the fee of £84 remains, plus the interment fee of £152; the cost is the same as if the service had been held in the church. No fee is payable for the burial of a stillborn child, or for the funeral or burial of an infant who died within one year of birth.

If, after cremation, the cremated remains or ashes are to be buried in the churchyard, the fee will be £76; there is no difference in the charge for burying ashes loose or in a casket. If the crematorium service has been a simple committal and the funeral service is to be held in the churchyard when the ashes are buried, a further fee of £84 is incurred – the same as for a service held in church. This fee does not apply, however, if the incumbent officiates at the burial of ashes elsewhere and provides a simple service of committal, when a fee of £30 is normally charged. This is the portion of the fee for burial of ashes in a churchyard that is paid directly to the incumbent.

Gravediggers' fees are in addition to the above. If the parish has its own gravedigger, the fee is likely to be less than £150; if the services of a professional gravedigger are required, the fee is likely to be between £150 and £300. These fees vary according to place and circumstances, and may rise annually – sometimes considerably.

The grave

Paying a burial fee does not buy the right to choose the location of the grave in the churchyard. The vicar allots the site. Nor does the burial fee entitle you to ownership of the grave or to the exclusive right of burial in that grave.

By faculty

If you want the exclusive use of a plot in a churchyard, you must apply to the diocesan registrar to reserve a grave space, by a licence called a faculty. Although a faculty gives the right to say who can be buried in the plot, the freehold of the ground continues to belong to the Church.

The fee charged by the diocese for a faculty depends on the amount of work involved in the petition. It takes about six weeks for a faculty to be granted. When a person dies, it is too late to get a faculty for him or her, but the relatives could apply for a faculty to reserve the grave for other members of the family. Anyone arranging a burial in a grave reserved by a faculty must produce the faculty or other evidence which proves his or her right to the grave.

The incumbent charges a fee for the first and each subsequent interment in a grave reserved by faculty. An additional charge is made for removing and replacing an existing headstone to enable subsequent interments in a grave to take place.

Burial inside a church

Today, any rights an incumbent may have had in the past to consent to a burial inside the church building have become obsolete. Faculties to permit such burials are rarely granted and in urban areas burial in and under a church is prohibited by law.

Burial at sea

Burial at sea is both complicated and expensive, but it is possible at certain places along the coast of the UK (see Chapter 17).

Other burial grounds

If you want to be buried in ground other than a churchyard or cemetery, the law stipulates that such private burials must be registered.

Woodland and green burials

In 1994 only one green burial site existed in England; now there are over 180, with many more planned. In Scotland, almost half of local authorities either provide woodland burial facilities, or are planning to do so. These burial grounds concentrate on keeping the environment as natural as possible, and plots are available in meadowland or woodland.

Normally no memorial stone or tablet is permitted, with memorials taking the form of a newly planted tree, sometimes with a name plaque. A number of woodland burial grounds will provide a complete, but simple burial service for about £1,000; if, however, a church service is required beforehand and a traditional hearse and limousines are provided, the cost will rise accordingly.

Where such services are supplied, all materials interred will be degradable and as natural as possible in order to encourage the wild nature of the environment. Rigid-based cardboard coffins are usually supplied or encouraged, and woven willow or bamboo coffins are becoming increasingly popular. Most burial authorities providing these services will be happy to supply advice (as will some local authorities through their websites). Costs and fees vary considerably, and further information should be obtained from the Natural Death Centre*.

Eco-friendly burial grounds

Since the introduction of the Charter for the Bereaved (see page 9), a growing number of environmental issues are gradually coming to the fore. Some burial authorities attempt to encourage as natural an environment as possible. This approach helps to maintain the peaceful character of the cemetery and fosters local flowers and wildlife. In burial grounds which adopt green practices, alternatives to memorial stones are encouraged, as much waste material as possible is composted, and less herbicide is used to maintain the grounds. Increasing tree planting can offset carbon dioxide emissions, and timber from lopped trees can be piled decoratively rather than being burnt. All of these moves, however, increase costs for labour and materials, which must be passed on to the clients in the form of increased charges for burials.

An increasing number of people are asking for charitable donations in place of flowers at funerals. Some would feel that a funeral with no flowers is very sad, but probably more would feel that the money spent on providing stacks of elaborate floral tributes, only to be left withering outside the crematorium, could be put to better use. The environmental damage caused by extensive production of cut flowers is also a cause for concern.

Burials on private land

No law prevents a burial taking place on private land, provided all the normal procedures of registration of the death have been completed, and the coroner, if involved, is satisfied that his or her investigations have also been completed. The Registrar of Births and Deaths will issue the normal green certificate, or the coroner will provide a coroner's certificate for burial; the detachable section (part C) must be completed by the person arranging the burial and returned to the registrar within 14 days of the funeral taking place.

If you are considering this option, a number of serious considerations must be taken into account:

- you must obtain permission from the owner of the land where the burial is to take place if it is not your own
- you must consult the local environmental health officer regarding the burial procedure and any possible effect it may have on nearby watercourses, and so on
- the presence of a grave on the property may reduce its value and make any future resale difficult
- you must inform any individual or mortgage company with an interest in the property of your intentions
- notification that a burial has taken place, together with an accurate map of the location, must be attached to the deeds of the property
- if you decide to move and want to remove the grave to a new location, a licence for exhumation must be obtained from the Home Office; professional assistance may be needed to deal with the exhumation.

Burial on farm land is an option which may be considered by some landowners; this may involve setting up a formal burial ground and require a long-term commitment to the project. Statutory requirements regarding the maintenance of burial records must be observed, and it would be wise to consult local planning authorities. Several such burial grounds have been established, and provide a valuable service to the local community.

Extending the use of existing cemeteries

In the face of an increasing shortage of burial space in existing cemeteries, certain suggestions have been made. Short-term solutions have included digging new graves between spaciously laid out nineteenth-century graves, reclaiming unused space in family graves after 75 years, and raising land by up to 20 feet in order to place new graves on top of old ones. However, all these options present problems: reclaiming unused space in family graves is expensive; raising the level of the land can lead to unpleasant high-rise graves; and digging up the flowerbeds of Victorian cemeteries can destroy their character.

In 1999, the Home Office issued a consultation document which recommended re-using old graves through a procedure known as 'lift and deepen'. This means re-opening an old grave, exhuming the remains, deepening the grave considerably and burying the exhumed remains much deeper than before. Up to five new burials can then occur on top. A study by Douglas Davies of Durham University which recommended the re-use of graves after 50 years found that 23 per cent of the public were in favour of re-using graves after this length of time, while 27 per cent were in favour of re-using graves after 75 years. When the 'lift and deepen' method was explained to participants in the survey, support for the system rose to 62 per cent.

The Office of Fair Trading report on funerals (July 2001) refers to an enquiry into the state of the nation's cemeteries by the Environment Sub-committee of the House of Commons Select Committee on the Environment, Transport and Regional Affairs. The Select Committee examined a number of issues including the condition of existing cemeteries, long-term planning for new cemeteries and burial space (including proposals for the re-use of graves), and the management and provision of cemetery services. The report of the Select Committee stressed the need to respect the significant minority preference for burial, and called upon local authorities to ensure the widest possible access to burial options, encouraging them to find ways of providing accessible local burial space.

In January 2004, the Home Office issued a consultation document entitled *Burial Law and Policy in the 21st Century: the Need for a Sensitive and Sustainable Approach*. This document seeks the views of relevant organisations and authorities on the revision of burial law, the provision of new cemeteries and the re-use of old cemeteries for new burials. The situation is becoming critical as more and more cemeteries run out of burial space and do not allow new burials, other than second interments in graves previously dug to double the normal depths. No reports have been issued at the time of going to press.

Chapter 11

Burial and cremation in Scotland

The certificate of registration of death which the registrar has given to the informant must be given to the person in charge of the place of interment or cremation. No part of the certificate is returned to the registrar.

Burial

In Scotland a grave is referred to as a lair. As in England, it is possible to purchase the exclusive right of burial in a cemetery or kirkyard plot, either in perpetuity or for a limited period. Cemeteries are administered by the local council. In Scotland, cemetery chapels are rare.

At burials in urban cemeteries, silk tasselled cords, called courtesy cords, are attached to the coffin. Specific mourners are sent a card beforehand inviting them to hold a cord while the coffin bearers take the strain of the lowering. In most areas of the country the cords actually take the weight. Courtesy cords are not used for the burial of cremated remains.

A pad or mattress is often put on top of the coffin as a development of the old custom of putting grass or straw over the coffin to muffle the sound of earth falling on the lid when the grave is filled in.

In Scotland by tradition women did not go to the interment in the graveyard after the church service. This practice has been abandoned by and large, although it still survives occasionally, especially in the older generation.

Cremation

The regulations and procedure for cremation are the same as in England and Wales since the Cremation Regulations 1965 brought these into line with those of Scotland.

Sending a body abroad

There are no formalities connected with the removal of bodies out of Scotland for either cremation or burial in another country, but you should ensure that the death has been registered in Scotland before moving the body out of Scotland. The procurator fiscal does not have to be informed.

If the body is being taken to England or Wales for burial, the certificate of registration (**Form 14**) or the standard death certificate must be produced for the registrar there.

No formal notice has to be given or permission sought when cremated remains are being taken out of the country.

Bringing a body from abroad

There is no need to produce evidence for the registrar in Scotland that the death took place elsewhere. If the body is coming from England or Wales, the person in charge of the place of interment or cremation in Scotland will require the coroner's form permitting the body to be removed.

When a body is brought into Scotland to be cremated there, the authority of the Scottish Ministers must be obtained before cremation can be carried out. This means applying to the Scottish Executive Health Department★, with any supporting papers, such as a foreign death certificate.

Cremated remains brought into Scotland must be accompanied by a certificate of cremation issued by the crematorium.

Chapter 12

Before the funeral

Most funeral directors maintain a 24-hour service; if a death occurs at home or in a nursing home out of office hours, two members of the funeral director's staff who are on duty at that time will come very quickly to take the body to the mortuary. Nursing and retirement homes normally want the body moved as soon as possible. It is rare, nowadays, for a body to remain at home for the interval between death and the funeral, although it is possible if the relatives request it. Unless the relatives intend arranging the funeral themselves, the funeral director should be approached as soon as possible after the death occurs. In many cases, the member of staff with whom you have the first interview will remain in charge until after the funeral is completed.

The body

By 1983, some 70 per cent of deaths took place in hospital; that percentage has now increased considerably. A further 10 per cent die in nursing homes, and most of the remainder in residential or private homes. The great majority of all these are taken to the funeral director's premises to await the funeral in a chapel of rest; this is a small room where the deceased remains in a coffin until shortly before the funeral. Laying out, or 'first offices' (known as 'last offices' in hospital), almost always takes place at the funeral director's mortuary. If the deceased is not to wear his or her own clothes, the funeral director will supply a funeral gown as part of the inclusive service. He or she will want to know what the family would like to do about any jewellery worn.

When someone dies in hospital, the body is normally taken to the hospital mortuary; however, a number of (usually small) hospitals now sub-contract mortuary facilities to a local funeral director. When a death occurs, the funeral director's staff will remove the body to his or her mortuary, where it will remain until cremation papers (if needed) have been completed. If the coroner is involved and decides that a post mortem is necessary, the funeral director's staff will take the body to the coroner's mortuary. The relatives are not obliged to make use of the services of this funeral director; he or she will co-operate with the funeral director chosen by the relatives.

If the body is taken to a mortuary on the hospital premises outside normal working hours, the hospital will not normally permit it to be moved until the next day. If the coroner is involved, the body cannot be moved until he or she is satisfied that the necessary papers can be issued.

When the funeral director's staff come to remove a body from a house or hospital, they normally use a large estate car adapted for the purpose. Sometimes an ambulance is used; very rarely, a hearse. The staff will normally use a covered stretcher; sometimes, a form of coffin designed for removals called a 'shell'. The funeral director usually needs written authority in order to remove a body from hospital; this normally takes the form of the green certificate issued by the registrar (registrar's certificate for burial or cremation), which means that registration must be attended to as soon as possible. An authorisation signed by the next of kin or executor is sometimes acceptable.

When the body is kept in a chapel of rest, relatives and friends can go to see it before the funeral; the funeral director will usually ask for an appointment to be made so that a member of staff can be available to give the family undivided attention. Sometimes extra charges are made for viewing the body at evenings or weekends. Relatives often like to leave some personal memento in the coffin, but are embarrassed to ask; funeral directors will often suggest that photographs, letters, flowers and so on may be placed in the coffin with the deceased. Where cremation is involved, it is important that these mementoes are combustible.

Some larger firms of funeral directors also have their own chapel for private prayer, in which a religious service can be held at the beginning of the funeral before the cortege leaves for the cemetery or crematorium.

Embalming

Embalming is a process intended to delay temporarily the process of decomposition, and involves replacing the blood in the arterial system with a preservative, normally a solution of formalin. The process is similar to a blood transfusion, and is sometimes called 'preservative' or 'hygienic' treatment. It bears no resemblance to the ancient Egyptian process of preserving bodies with spices, resulting in mummification, and has no long-term preservative value.

Embalming is advisable if the body is to be returned to a private house to await the funeral, or if the funeral is to be held more than four or five days from the date of death and the body cannot be kept in cold storage. Some bodies begin to decompose much sooner than others: if the deceased person required a high intake of certain drugs during a terminal illness, the body can deteriorate rapidly. Some funeral directors feel that all bodies should be embalmed, but permission for embalming should always be obtained from the next of kin or executor after a full discussion.

While some families have no wish to visit their deceased relatives in the funeral director's chapel of rest, for others this is very important, and can assist considerably with the grief process; however, a bad appearance and odours can be extremely distressing. If the funeral director feels that embalming is advisable, he or she should discuss the matter with those arranging the funeral, who should make their preference clear if they do not want the body of their relative to be embalmed. Sometimes there is an extra charge for embalming.

In some burial schemes, such as woodland burial (see page 94), all chemicals may be prohibited; this restriction may apply to the use of embalming fluid as well as to the use of horticultural chemicals at the burial site. A 'green' embalming fluid is now available, and is gradually coming into use among embalmers. It excludes harmful and toxic chemicals and is based on organic ingredients.

Before a body can be embalmed the doctor must have completed the medical certificate of the cause of death, and the death must have been registered. Where cremation is involved, **Forms B** and **C** must also have been completed (see Chapter 9). If the coroner is involved, embalming must not take place until his or her authority has been obtained. An embalmer should be qualified by examination, and abide by the code of practice laid down by the British Institute of Embalmers. In the UK, embalmers tend to make minimal use of cosmetics (unless requested otherwise by the family); the aim is to present as natural an appearance as possible, as if the deceased were asleep.

In a hospital mortuary, the bodies are kept refrigerated; most funeral directors also have cold-storage facilities, sometimes combined with deep-freeze facilities so that bodies can, if necessary, be kept for some considerable time before the funeral takes place. This may be necessary where a member of the family is abroad and cannot be contacted or where a close relative is in hospital awaiting recovery.

Final arrangements

The funeral director must have the registrar's green certificate (or the coroner's equivalent authorisation) before confirming the final arrangements. He or she will see to it that all official forms are completed and taken to the right people at the right time. For a burial, for instance, he or she takes charge of any grave deeds and gets a cemetery's form of application signed by the executor.

In effect, the funeral director should co-ordinate the various operations at the different stages. He or she will approach the people in charge of wherever it has been decided the burial or cremation is to take place (this usually means the local clergyman or superintendent of the cemetery or crematorium) in order to reserve a time and, for a burial, to order the type of grave required.

For a cremation, the funeral director sees that a relative or the executor completes the form of application and the form giving instructions for disposal of the ashes and will also arrange for two doctors to complete **Forms B** and **C**. He or she will pay them their fees and, when the necessary forms have been gathered, will pass them to the medical referee at the crematorium.

Most crematoria produce at least one other form on which the person organising the funeral confirms any details already provisionally arranged, such as the date and time of cremation. Some crematoria ask on this form for specific instructions about the disposal of the ashes; others have yet another form for this.

The forms have to be submitted to the medical referee of the crematorium by a stipulated time – which is never less than 24 hours before the cremation is due. The reservation of a time for the cremation is accepted subject to the forms reaching the crematorium within the specified time limit and the fees being paid in advance.

The fees – to vicar, gravedigger, organist, choirmaster, chaplain and officials at the cemetery or crematorium (and to doctors for cremation papers, where cremation is involved) – usually have to be paid in advance. The funeral director will make the actual payments on behalf of his or her clients and will add the charges to the total account; increasingly, funeral directors require these disbursement charges to be paid at the time of arranging the funeral.

Arranging the funeral service

Either the funeral director or a member of the family should speak to whoever the family wants to officiate at the service, and find out whether he or she is willing to do so and is available at the time planned for holding the ceremony. Mostly, a minister of religion is involved, who should contact the family, visiting them whenever possible, in order to offer consolation and arrange practical details of the service. Most people feel that a funeral service should be intensely personal, and whoever conducts the service will need to talk with the family so that a fitting tribute to the deceased can be made effectively. The person conducting the funeral service does not have to be a minister of religion; increasingly, funeral services are conducted by a representative of one of the humanist organisations, an experienced funeral director, or a friend of the family.

Church of England funeral services

A Church of England funeral service that is held in church may be conducted by the incumbent or, with his or her permission, by any other clergyman – for instance, the clergyman whose church the deceased normally attended or who is a member or friend of the family.

There is no obligation to hold a service in church; unlike weddings, for which a building or location must be licensed through the registration authority, funeral services may be held in any building, or at the graveside. Increasingly, funeral services involving cremation are held in the crematorium chapel, but if this is not large enough, the service may be held in a village hall or any such suitable building, with only the committal taking place at the crematorium. There is a growing tendency for the whole service, including the committal, to take place at the church or hall; the coffin is then taken away to the crematorium with only one or two direct family members attending as witnesses. Sometimes this procedure is reversed: there is a private committal at the crematorium early in the day, attended by a few family members, and the funeral service proper is held in a church or hall later in the day.

The local vicar or rector will be accustomed to taking funeral services in crematorium chapels, and may be prevailed upon to conduct such services in other locations. This may be an advantage if a longer form of funeral service is planned, as services in most crematoria are limited to about 20 to 25 minutes, although double time may usually be booked at an extra charge.

The Church of England, in common with most religious denominations, has a form of funeral ceremony, but again, unlike weddings, there is no legal requirement for any form of words to be said. In the UK, unless the dead person had professed another religion, or the relatives have made specific requests, one of the Church of England orders of funeral service will probably be said at the funeral. Most rituals can be adapted according to the preferences of those concerned. For instance, the main part of the service can be held in the church or some other suitable building, with only a few words of committal at the graveside or crematorium, or the whole service can be held where the committal is to take place. A funeral address may be given either in the church or outside, or not at all.

Many people give a lot of thought to planning the kind of funeral service they would like for their deceased relatives, with readings, poetry and particular pieces of music. Services held in a Church of England church may be more limited due to the liturgical constraints felt by some of the clergy. Most crematoria have facilities for playing recorded music, and those who would prefer music of their own choice in the funeral service or when entering or leaving should ask for this when making arrangements for the service. If an unusual form of funeral service is planned, special service sheets may be printed; these may be obtained through the funeral director, directly from a local printer, or produced at home by anyone with a computer.

Non-Church of England funerals

Denominational burial grounds usually insist on their own form of service. If you are arranging the funeral of someone of a faith different from your own, get in touch as soon as possible with the equivalent of the local parish priest of that denomination to find out what needs to be done. (See also Chapter 14.)

For a practising Roman Catholic, it is usual to arrange for the priest to say a requiem mass in the local parish church and for him to take the funeral service. A requiem mass in a Roman Catholic church will follow a very precise order. There are no set fees laid down for Roman Catholic priests to charge for funeral services, but it is usual for the deceased's family to make an offering to the church. Cremation is no longer discouraged for Roman Catholics, and crematoria have Roman Catholic priests on their roster, where such rosters are used.

With Orthodox Jews, the body should be buried as soon as possible once the disposal certificate is issued. If a man subscribes to a synagogue burial society, he or his wife or his dependent children will be buried, free, by the society in its cemetery. The funeral and coffin will be very simple, and there will be no flowers. Orthodox Jews are never cremated, and embalming or bequeathing a body for medical purposes is not allowed. Reform non-orthodox Jews are more flexible, and permit cremation. The funeral will always be simple, but flowers are allowed. A Jewish burial society may agree to carry out the funeral of a Jew who was not a member of a synagogue and had not been subscribing to any burial society, but his family will be charged for the funeral and the cost will be considerable. There is rarely any difference between the funeral of members of the same synagogue; all are simple. If a Jew dies when away from home, it is the responsibility of the relatives to bring the body back at their own expense for the synagogue burial society to take over.

Non-religious services

There is no necessity to have a religious ceremony, or indeed any kind of ceremony at all, at a funeral. A 2001 report from the British Humanist Association* revealed that more non-religious funerals are conducted in England and Wales than in most other European nations put together. However, because some kind of religious ceremony is customary, if you do not want one or the dead person had made it clear that he or she did not want one, it is important that the executor or whoever is in charge of the arrangements makes this known well before the funeral.

If a body is to buried in a churchyard without a religious ceremony, or with a ceremony held by an officiant of another denomination, you should give the incumbent of the parish 48 hours' notice in writing; in practice, it should be possible to make the necessary arrangements in a telephone conversation. The usual parish regulations and fees still apply, and additional fees for the officiant may be involved.

If a body is to be buried in a cemetery or cremated at a crematorium without a religious ceremony, tell the funeral director or the authorities at the time the funeral is being arranged. There will normally be no difficulties, provided it is clear that the proceedings will be properly conducted. Where there is not going to be a religious ceremony, whoever is in charge of the funeral arrangements must also make arrangements for the details of the ceremony.

If you want no ceremony at all, the usual procedure is for a few members of the family or close friends to attend the committal in silence or with some music being played. If you want a non-religious ceremony without an officiant, on the lines of a Society of Friends (Quaker) meeting, you must make sure that those present either know already how such a ceremony works or are told at the beginning.

The more usual procedure is to have an officiant who prepares and conducts the ceremony, on the lines of a minister. This may be a member of the family or a close friend, or a representative of an appropriate organisation or a sympathetic religious minister. The only qualification is some experience of handling meetings. Business, professional and labour organisations generally contain such people, as do humanist societies.

The national freethought organisations in London and elsewhere all give help with funerals: they can offer information and advice by telephone or post, send out literature, and sometimes provide officiants for funerals. The British Humanist Association* has a network of humanist funeral officiants who can be contacted by calling the 24-hour national helpline; its accredited officiants conducted some 4,800 funerals in 2000, and the number has been rising by an average of 40 per cent each year. Other agencies include the National Secular Society★, the Rationalist Press Association★ and the South Place Ethical Society★. The booklet *Funerals without God: A Practical Guide to Non-religious Funerals* can be obtained from the British Humanist Association, and the other organisations can provide literature for which donations would be appreciated. Officiants at funerals would expect to be paid a standard fee plus travelling expenses; these are normally about the same as fees set for church ministers.

It will also be possible in some areas for an experienced funeral director to conduct the service. In the circumstances surrounding a funeral arrangement, trusting relationships are often formed very quickly, and some people feel they would rather be helped in this way by the funeral director than someone whom they do not know.

A non-religious ceremony may take any form, provided it is decent and orderly. The usual procedure is for the officiant to explain the ceremony, after which there may be readings of appropriate prose or poetry, tributes either by the officiant or others present, and the playing of appropriate music. It is common to allow a time of silence when the deceased may be remembered personally, and religious people may offer silent prayers. These ceremonies are not intended to oppose religious funerals, but are alternatives for people who would feel it hypocritical to have a religious service, or who want a respectful celebration of the death that has occurred without a religious emphasis.

Press notices

Announcements of deaths are usually made in local papers, and sometimes the national dailies; the cost for an average obituary in a local paper is likely to be about £80, and in a national paper about £150–£300. Newspapers will not normally accept text for obituaries by telephone, unless placed by a funeral director; even then there is a rigorous callback and checking system because of many distressing hoaxes. The papers do not usually ask for evidence that the death has occurred, unless the notice is submitted by someone who is not a relative, executor or funeral director.

National daily newspapers prefer a standard form of announcement, and are likely to restrict the format and words that can be used. Most funeral directors are well aware of the system, and will advise accordingly. The address of the deceased should *not* be inserted into the obituary: too many houses have been burgled while the funeral is taking place. Where there is anxiety about this, the funeral director may be able to supply a member of staff as a 'house sitter' for the duration of the funeral service.

The majority of funerals currently give people the opportunity of making donations to a nominated charity in memory of the deceased, as well as, or in place of, flowers. It is normal for the funeral director to collect such donations and forward them in due course to the charity concerned, informing the relatives of the amount collected. This information is usually contained in the obituary, and the funeral director's name and address are given so that information can be given and donations made.

Details of the date, time and place of the funeral can be included in the obituary. Anyone who has not been specifically invited but wishes to attend is expected to arrive independently at the time and place announced in the press. If the family wants to restrict attendance at the funeral, the obituary should state 'private funeral service', or the equivalent; in this case, only those invited by the family should attend. If the family think that a great many people may wish to attend, arrangements may be made for a funeral service in a large church or auditorium followed by cremation or burial which is attended only by the family and close friends; alternatively, a private funeral for the family only may be followed some time later by a memorial service and all who wish to pay their last respects to the deceased may attend. If no details of the time or place are published, it should be assumed that the funeral is to be private.

Flowers

The press notice should make clear whether there are to be no flowers, family flowers only, or the option of a memorial donation. A 'no flowers' request should be strictly observed. Flowers are normally sent to the funeral director's premises; most florists are aware of this, and will contact the funeral director to ask what time flowers should be delivered. It is not normal for press notices nowadays to say where flowers should be sent: the funeral director will collect any that are sent to the family home when he or she calls at the house for the funeral service, and will normally supply the family with a list of those who sent flowers when submitting the account. Flower cards may be collected and returned if the funeral director is asked to do so.

When a body is buried, flowers are normally left on the grave after it has been filled in. At the crematorium, there will normally be restrictions as to where flowers can be placed, and the length of time they will be displayed: some are on display for only 24 hours after the funeral and others for a week or more. Traditional wreaths are rare nowadays; it is common for the family to request flowers in the form of bouquets or arrangements that can be taken to hospitals or old people's homes after the funeral service has been completed.

Chapter 13

The funeral service

Traditionally, the cortege (or funeral procession) started at the house where the deceased lived, with the hearse and one or more cars for the mourners travelling by a pre-arranged route to the church or crematorium. This still frequently happens, but it is as common for the hearse to travel directly to the location of the funeral from the funeral director's premises; the mourners will then be brought to meet it by either their own or the funeral director's vehicles. If the funeral director provides cars for the bereaved relatives, he or she will marshal the cortege and arrange its departure.

Timing is most important, because cemetery and cremation authorities work to a very tight schedule; if the funeral cortege arrives too early or too late, it will probably interfere with the preceding or following funerals. Should it arrive considerably late, especially at the crematorium, it is possible that the funeral service will have to be drastically shortened, or even postponed, to the great distress of the relatives.

The funeral director should have discussed all the details of the funeral with the family beforehand, and arranged where people are to be taken after the funeral, whether the minister requires transport, what happens to the flowers and so on.

If you are worried that the house may be burgled while the funeral is taking place, the funeral director may be able to provide a member of staff as a 'house sitter'. The funeral director should not incur any additional expenses without the client's authority.

It is unlikely nowadays that the funeral director will ask relatives if they would like to witness the closing of the coffin immediately before the funeral, but customs vary in different parts of the UK.

The funeral director may walk in front of the hearse as it leaves the deceased's house, and again as it approaches the church or crematorium; this is not only as a mark of respect, but to enable him or her to direct the traffic and keep the funeral cortege together, especially as it leaves a side street to enter a main road. The coffin is traditionally carried into the church or crematorium on the shoulders of four of the funeral director's staff, although in some places a small trolley is used for moving the coffin. At the time of writing, discussions taking place with the Health and Safety Executive have raised serious questions about possible back injury while lifting and carrying coffins on the shoulders, and it is possible that this practice may be curtailed for professional staff.

When members or friends of the family are able to act as bearers, this makes for a closer participation in the funeral, and the funeral director's staff will still be on hand to assist and give directions. Occasionally, at more formal funerals, pall-bearers walk alongside the coffin, apparently fulfilling no purpose. Traditionally, these used to carry the 'pall', a heavy fabric canopy which was held over the coffin. Today, the pall is normally used to cover the coffin in the hearse if it has to travel some considerable distance between towns before the funeral cortege can gather; it is then removed, and the family flowers are placed on the coffin before it moves off.

Burial

Where a burial is preceded by a church service, the coffin is taken into the church by the bearers and placed on trestles or a trolley in front of the altar. In Roman Catholic and some other churches, the coffin may be taken into church before the funeral, often the previous evening, and remain there until the funeral service takes place. Most funeral services in church take about half an hour, although a requiem mass, or the funeral of a well-known member of the church congregation, may take an hour or more. After the service, the bearers will take the coffin from the church, either to the churchyard or, more commonly, to the local cemetery, usually led by the minister and funeral director. If burial is not preceded by a church service, the coffin is carried direct from the hearse to the graveside, where there is normally a short service.

The coffin will be lowered into the grave by the bearers while the words of committal are said; this part of the funeral service is quite brief, and normally lasts about five minutes. In Scotland, the coffin is usually lowered by members of the family. Sometimes the mourners throw a token handful of earth into the grave, or each drops a flower on to the coffin; they do not normally (except in Ireland) remain to see the grave filled in – this is done later by the cemetery staff or gravedigger.

A register of burials in the parish is kept by the church; every cemetery has to keep a register of burials and records of who owns a grave plot, and who has already been buried in each grave. Copies of the entries in these registers can be obtained for a small fee.

When someone is buried in a Church of England churchyard the family is responsible for looking after the grave. The PCC (parochial church council) is responsible for looking after the churchyard generally, and for keeping the paths and unused parts tidy. Some dioceses stipulate that, before a funeral takes place, a contribution must be made towards the upkeep of the churchyard. Municipal and private cemeteries will employ groundsmen to take care of grounds and graves; this upkeep is often difficult and costly, which is why most authorities now stipulate lawn graves only: graves with a simple headstone in line with other headstones, and no kerbs or surrounds to interfere with mechanical mowing. However, where there are gravestones, whether simple or elaborate, the holder of the grave deeds is responsible for their upkeep; this can become very expensive as stones weather and crack, and ground settles over the years. Upkeep of memorial stones is often neglected – another reason why authorities prefer to stipulate lawn graves only.

Many churches place quite rigid restrictions on the type of memorials and stone which may be used in churchyards. It is essential to check with the local church before placing an order with a stonemason; funeral directors will be aware of the requirements of local churches and will be able to advise accordingly.

Cremation

Traditionally, the funeral service prior to cremation was held in church, with the congregation (or only the chief mourners if the cremation was to be private) travelling to the appropriate crematorium for a brief committal afterwards. Increasingly, funeral services are held entirely in crematorium chapels; the hearse and cars go straight to the crematorium and the bearers carry the coffin into the chapel and place it on the catafalque. Usually, the mourners follow the coffin into the crematorium, led by the minister and funeral director but, increasingly, people prefer to enter the chapel and sit down before the coffin is brought in, or have the coffin brought in before the mourners arrive. This is difficult in crematoria, as access to the crematorium chapel is not possible until mourners at the previous funeral have left. However, it is usually possible for the coffin to be in place before the main mourners arrive.

When the words of committal are spoken, the coffin passes out of sight; it will either sink into a recess or pass through a door, or a curtain will move in front of it. Some people prefer the coffin to remain on the catafalque until the mourners have left the chapel; this option is available if requested. During the funeral service, the funeral director's staff will take flowers from the hearse and place them in the floral display area; when the coffin moves out of sight at committal, the flowers on the coffin will be retrieved and added to the display. Some crematoria will only keep flowers on display for the day following the funeral; others leave them in place for several days, while yet others clear them once a week. The funeral director will take appropriate sprays and arrangements to hospitals or nursing homes if requested: these are often greatly appreciated.

When the coffin moves out of sight, it is taken to the committal room to await cremation. Each coffin is loaded individually into a cremator, once the name on the coffin plate has been checked by the crematorium staff. It is illegal to remove the coffin from the crematorium, or (other than the flowers) anything from the coffin, once the committal has been made. When the cremation process is complete, after two or three hours, the ashes are refined separately and placed in carefully labelled containers; each cremator must be cleared before another coffin can be loaded.

When making arrangements for the cremation, the next of kin or executors can ask to be present when the coffin is placed in the cremator; this is especially relevant for Hindu funerals, where traditionally the next of kin would light the funeral pyre. Usually, two people only are allowed.

Each crematorium has to keep a register of cremations. A copy of the entry in the register is obtainable for a small fee.

Disposal of the ashes

When making arrangements for the funeral, the clients will be asked what they would like done with the ashes. Most are scattered, or buried loose beneath the turf in the crematorium grounds; they can, however, be taken away by the next of kin or executor for disposal elsewhere, for example, scattering in a place meaningful to the deceased or family, or burial in a churchyard or cemetery. If they are taken away, the crematorium provides a free certificate (usually required by churchyards or cemeteries) confirming that the cremation has taken place. If a family grave already exists, the ashes may be buried in that grave for a fee, usually around £70. If a plot for the burial of ashes has to be purchased (i.e. where no family grave exists), there will (except in churchyards) be a fee for the exclusive right of burial. Cremated remains can usually be obtained from the crematorium on the day following the funeral; however, providing notice is given in advance, ashes may be obtained on the same day if the funeral takes place before midday.

Crematoria are sometimes unwilling to post or otherwise send cremated remains to other locations. However, most funeral directors will take them short distances by car or arrange for national transportation by a courier. It is difficult and expensive to send them by post yourself but if you wish to do so you should consult one of the national parcel services. Costs are usually between £20 and £30 inland, and more to any UK islands.

Most crematoria, for a monthly fee, will arrange to store ashes until they are required; funeral directors will do the same, but most will probably not charge for storage. Funeral directors will also supply caskets for burial of ashes, or simple urns for storage or scattering. These vary in price from about £15 for a simple urn to several hundred pounds for an elaborate casket. Decisions about or arrangements for the eventual disposal of ashes need not be made at the time of the funeral. However, if there is even the remotest likelihood that the crematorium will *not* be required to scatter the ashes in its grounds, this should be made clear at the outset. It is easy to scatter ashes later, but, obviously, impossible to do anything else with them once they have been scattered. Normally, when signing statutory **Form A** (see page 79), the next of kin or executor must fill in a form on the reverse giving instructions for the ashes.

If ashes are to be scattered in the grounds of a different crematorium, or the same crematorium at a considerably later date, there will be an additional fee of around £30. If a funeral director has to arrange for ashes to be buried in a different location or at a considerably later time, he or she will charge a fee in addition to the inclusive fee for the funeral. There is no law regarding the scattering of cremated remains; ashes can be scattered anywhere, providing that this is done respectfully, and with the consent of the owners or executors of private grounds, such as golf courses, and so on. The funeral director will arrange to scatter the ashes for clients in a chosen location and will not normally charge for this unless considerable time and travelling expenses are incurred.

The crematorium grounds are usually known as a 'Garden of Remembrance'; such ground is not usually consecrated, and the place where ashes are scattered is not normally marked. Some crematoria scatter the ashes around on the surface of the grass or earth; others remove a small portion of turf, pour the ashes on the ground and then replace the turf. Some allow a casket containing the ashes to be buried in the grounds. The family can choose a spot and witness the proceedings if they request to do so; some crematoria charge a fee for this. There is generally no formal ceremony for the scattering of ashes; the burial of a casket is, however, frequently attended by a minister who conducts a brief service of committal.

Parish churches of the Church of England will frequently allow only ashes to be buried in churchyards, as there is little room left for full burials; fees for this are £76 in 2005. Most churches will allow the placement of a small stone plaque, inscribed with the name of the deceased, where the ashes are buried. As with headstones, there are usually rigid restrictions about the type and size of stone that is accepted. Each church tends to have its own interpretation of regulations, and it is essential that enquiries are made at the appropriate church as to what memorials are allowed before the interment takes place; church stipulations may not be acceptable to the relatives. A fee will be charged for placing the memorial stone, in either a churchyard or cemetery.

A final word: if a decision is taken to scatter the ashes, and this is to be carried out by the family, it is important to ensure that the mourners stand with the wind behind them.

Chapter 14

Non-Christian and minority group funerals

In today's multi-ethnic society, and especially in inner-city areas, many funerals do not conform to the traditional Christian approach that has been the main emphasis of this book so far. This chapter briefly and simply outlines the practices of other faiths, of which there are now large numbers of adherents throughout the UK.

Muslims

Muslims live according to a strict moral code which has specific prescriptions concerning death and burial. There are numerous Muslim sects, each with its own variation of funeral rites, but in the UK about 90 per cent are Sunni Muslims, and the remaining 10 per cent are almost entirely Shia Muslims.

Muslim communities normally appoint one person to represent them in making funeral arrangements, who will usually deal with one approved funeral director in the locality. The representative will advise on the rules, which are strict and need to be followed as closely as possible.

Muslims are always buried, never cremated. Traditionally, there is no coffin – the body is wrapped in a plain white sheet and buried within 24 hours of death in an unmarked grave, which must be raised between 4 inches and 12 inches from the ground, and must not be walked, sat or stood upon. Most cemeteries in Britain, however, require a coffin for burial or cremation. Many British cemeteries insist on levelling the graves as soon as possible, which has led to some authorities providing special areas for Muslim burials; where there is none, families can suffer great distress. Because of the need for haste in burials, requests for post mortems and organ donation are usually, but not always, refused.

Muslims believe that the soul remains for some time in the body after death, and the body remains conscious of pain. Bodies must therefore be handled with great care and sensitivity, and disposable gloves worn at all times by those handling the body: the body must never be touched directly by a non-Muslim. Embalming is not normally practised, but is permissible where the body has to be conveyed over long distances.

Normally, the family will attend to laying out the body, and they will turn the head over the right shoulder to face Mecca, which in the UK is roughly to the south-east. The body will be wrapped in a plain sheet and taken home or to the mosque for ritual washing: men will wash male bodies, and women female. Camphor is normally placed in the armpits and body orifices, and the body will be dressed in clean white cotton clothes or a special white shroud brought back personally from Mecca.

The funeral service will take considerable time. There will be ritual washing, at least 30 minutes of prayer at the mosque, possible return to the family home, prayers at the graveside and the filling in of the grave. Relatives and friends will carry the coffin at shoulder height, passing it from one to another, and they will want to see the face of the deceased after the final prayer at the graveside. Muslims must be buried facing Mecca, with the head over the right shoulder; hence graves must lie north-east/south-west, with the head at the south-west end. The family will normally perform all rites and ceremonies, together with the imam, the spiritual leader of the local mosque.

Hindus

Hindus, unlike Muslims, do not normally insist on one approved funeral director to handle funerals; there is no central authority for those who adhere to this religion, and rites and customs vary enormously.

There are thousands of Hindu deities, which are all held to be manifestations of the same God. The three main deities are Brahma, the Creator; Vishnu, the Preserver; and Shiva, the Destroyer. Hindu belief in reincarnation means that most individuals face death in the hope of achieving a better form in the next round of life. Death is therefore relatively insignificant, although there is likely to be open mourning with much weeping and physical contact by the family and friends. There are normally strong objections to post mortem examinations, which are held to be deeply disrespectful to the dead.

Hindus are always cremated, and never buried. Prior to the cremation, most Hindus bring their dead into a chapel of rest, where the body must be wrapped in a plain sheet and placed on the floor. Most light lamps or candles, and those who come to view will probably burn incense sticks. There are normally no objections to the body being handled by non-Hindus, but this and all burial rites are capable of great variation. The family concerned will be explicit about the rites required by their form of Hinduism. The Asian Funeral Service★ arranges Hindu funerals and organises repatriation for those who require a funeral by the Ganges.

Sikhs

Sikhism developed from Hinduism in the fifteenth century and has much in common with it, but with a strong emphasis on militarism. There is a common belief in reincarnation, and the fact of death is normally accepted calmly.

There are five symbols of faith which are vitally important to every Sikh. The *Kesh* is the uncut hair which, for men, is always turbaned. The *Kangha* is a ritual comb to keep the hair in place; this is never removed. The *Kara* is a steel bracelet worn on the right wrist (or left if left-handed); the *Kirpan* is a small symbolic dagger, which may actually vary in size from a brooch to a broadsword – and the Sikh will never be separated from it. Finally, the *Kaccha* are ceremonial undergarments which are never completely removed, even while bathing. Sikhs are always cremated, never buried; the Sikh family will insist in every instance that their dead are cremated with all five 'K symbols' present. Considerable diplomacy may be required to satisfy both family and crematorium authorities.

After death, men are dressed in a white cotton shroud and turban; young women are dressed in red, and older women in white. The family will almost always want to lay out the body, and will want cremation to take place as soon as possible – in India, it would normally be within 24 hours. The coffin will normally be taken home and opened for friends and family to pay their last respects and will then be taken either to the *gurdwara*, for the main funeral service, or direct to the crematorium, where the oldest son will, instead of lighting the traditional funeral pyre, press the crematorium button or see the coffin into the cremator. The ashes will be required for scattering in a river or at sea; it is not unusual for one member of the family to take them to India to scatter them in the Punjab.

Stillborn babies, by exception, are usually buried.

Buddhists

Buddhism is the main religion in many Far-Eastern countries such as Burma and Nepal, but it is still relatively rare in the UK. After death, Buddhists will have the deceased person wrapped in a plain sheet and prepared for cremation. Buddhists of different nationalities have widely varying funeral customs, and nothing can be assumed to be held in common.

Jews

Scattered from their homeland by the Roman army in AD 70, the Jews dispersed across the world and adopted many different practices and interpretations of the Mosaic Law, yet always maintaining their essential unity. Orthodox Jews believe that the Law was literally handed to Moses by God, while Progressive Jews (divided into Reform, Liberal and Conservative groups) believe that the Law, while inspired, was written down and influenced by many different authors. Orthodox Jews are therefore extremely strict on the observation of funeral rites, while Progressive Jews vary in their attitudes.

When a Jew dies, the body is traditionally left for eight minutes while a feather is placed on the mouth and nostrils to give any indications or signs of breathing. Eyes and mouth are then closed by the oldest son, or nearest relative. Many Jews follow the custom of appointing 'wachers': people who stay with the body night and day until the funeral, praying and reciting psalms. The dead are buried as soon as possible. No Orthodox Jew will accept cremation, although it is becoming increasingly favourable among some Progressive groups. Orthodox rabbis will sometimes permit the burial of cremated remains in a full-sized coffin, and say *Kaddish* (the mourner's prayer) for the person concerned.

Jewish funerals are usually arranged by a Jewish funeral agency (such as United Synagogues). Otherwise, the local Jewish community will arrange a contract with a Gentile funeral service, under which all Jewish funerals will be carried out according to strict rabbinical control. If a secular Jew is appointed as executor, or is responsible for making funeral arrangements, it is essential that enquiries are made into the religious background of the deceased, so that the appropriate rabbi may be contacted.

Jewish coffins are as simple and plain as possible, usually with rope handles and written nameplates. Embalming does not take place, and mourners do not view the body.

The Jewish Bereavement Counselling Service★ offers support to those who have lost loved ones.

Cults

There are now a great variety of Christian cults, or diverging Christian groups, which include the Mormons, Jehovah's Witnesses, Christadelphians, Christian Scientists, Scientologists, the Moonies and the Children of God. For most, while differences in doctrine are held to be immensely important, there is little deviation from orthodox Christian practice as far as funerals are concerned. Funerals may well take longer, however, which may cause difficulties in fitting in with crematorium schedules.

Some groups, such as Bahai and Hare Krishna, are basically Hindu derivants, and may adhere more closely to Hindu funeral rites than any other.

Much New Age culture is basically a westernised form of Hinduism, and those who practise yoga or transcendental meditation may adopt the Hindu philosophies which lie behind them, which will in due course affect the funeral arrangements that will need to be made.

Chapter 15

Arranging a funeral without a funeral director

Many people assume that funerals can only be carried out by professional funeral directors, but it is quite possible for those who want to organise the funeral themselves to do so. Details given in the Charter for the Bereaved (see page 9) supply sufficient information to enable people to undertake their own arrangements.

Generally, when a close relative or friend dies most people prefer someone outside the immediate family circle to undertake responsibility for the funeral arrangements and to attend to all the necessary details. Many want to 'get the funeral over with' as soon as possible, and are reluctant to be involved any more than is necessary in making arrangements for, and participating in, the funeral service. However, human reactions to grief follow a fairly standard pattern (see Chapter 18), and it is an established fact that personal involvement in arrangements for the funeral will assist the grieving process and, for most, hasten a healthy recovery.

Such participation will, for most people, seldom involve more than laying out and dressing the deceased, visiting the deceased in the chapel of rest, providing family bearers to carry the coffin and participating in the funeral service. It is, however, perfectly possible to arrange the whole funeral yourself. The funeral director normally organises the funeral by collecting and moving the body of the deceased person, washing, dressing and sometimes embalming the body, attending to any necessary hygienic arrangements, and providing a coffin, chapel of rest, a hearse and staff to carry out the funeral. All of these tasks can be dealt with by the relatives, and while there can be considerable snags and difficulties, with knowledge and determination these can be overcome.

Arranging the funeral

Assuming that the coroner is not involved, the doctor's medical certificate of the cause of death must be obtained, and the death registered. A decision as to whether the funeral will involve burial or cremation must be taken. The necessary papers must be obtained, completed and submitted to the cemetery or crematorium with the appropriate fees. A date and time for the funeral must be arranged with the same authorities – if a church service is to be held, the church and minister must be consulted before that time is confirmed. If a minister is to conduct the service, he or she must be asked to do so, again before confirming the time. A coffin will normally be required, and a decision must be made about where the body is to be kept until the time of the funeral service. If the death occurred in a hospital or nursing home, some means of collecting the body of the deceased must be obtained, and also of conveying the coffin to the church, crematorium or cemetery.

If the funeral is to involve burial, and the cemetery or churchyard does not provide an inclusive gravedigging service, a gravedigger must be hired, or a family member or friend has to dig the grave. This should be considered very carefully, as many cemeteries may be located on heavy clay or stony ground, the digging of which can be extremely difficult. If the grave is to be on private land, the environmental health officer must be consulted. Bearers must be found to carry the coffin. These details constitute the necessary minimum: several of the above details involve forms which take time and patience to obtain and process.

Cremation

Cremation is much more common than burial – currently, at least 72 per cent of funerals involve cremation. If you have decided that the funeral you are arranging is going to involve cremation, you must first obtain two doctors' certificates to enable the cremation to take place. These are **Forms B** and **C**, normally printed on the same piece of paper; you may need to obtain a form from a crematorium or funeral director – most, but not all, doctors will have their own supply. If the death occurred in hospital, you must ask the hospital for the papers; if the death occurred at home or in a nursing home, the doctor who had been attending the person who died will complete **Form B**, and another independent doctor will complete **Form C**. A standard fee for the completion of each form will be charged (£55.50 per form in 2005). If the deceased was fitted with a cardiac pacemaker, this must be removed, normally by the hospital or the doctor completing **Form B**; the doctor will be paid for this separately, probably by the appropriate Primary Care Trust, and no charge should now be passed on to the client.

The next of kin or executor will need to obtain statutory **Form A** from the crematorium; this is the application for cremation, and it will be accompanied by the crematorium's own administration form giving details of the service required. Both must be completed and submitted to the crematorium with the doctors' **Forms B** and **C**, the registrar's green certificate for burial or cremation and the appropriate fee. If the coroner has been involved, **Forms B** and **C** will be replaced by the coroner's **Form E** for cremation; otherwise the documentation remains the same. The documents required for cremation are described in Chapter 9.

Most crematoria insist that a coffin be used (for the exceptions, consult the Natural Death Centre)★. The crematorium's administration form will include a signed declaration that the coffin conforms to legislation relating to pollution of the environment. This is important: people have in the past constructed coffins for loved ones and brought them to the crematorium only to be refused permission to cremate because the coffins did not conform to the necessary requirements. These requirements are usually printed on the crematorium's application form, and can be obtained from the local crematorium.

Burial

Burial has fewer problems than cremation, provided it is to take place in a churchyard or cemetery. No doctors' certificates (**Forms B** and **C**) are required, but the registrar's green certificate for burial or cremation (see page 30) must be submitted to the church or cemetery authorities, together with, in the case of a municipal or private cemetery, a completed application form and the required fee. A date and time for the funeral must be agreed. If necessary, a gravedigger must be found and hired: however, the churchyard or cemetery may provide the services of a gravedigger.

Coffin

For those with the ability, it is possible to construct a suitable coffin at home. It must be strong enough to cope with the stress imparted by an inert body being carried and lowered by inexpert bearers, and be made of suitable material: some cemeteries will not allow the burial of any metallic coffin or casket. In the case of cremation, the coffin must be made of materials that conform to the specifications laid down by the crematorium; these are usually printed on the application form, and it is normal practice for a signature indicating compliance to be required. A reasonable degree of expertise and experience are required: it is far from funny when a coffin collapses at a funeral, and no one should contemplate beginning a DIY career by making a coffin.

Coffins can be purchased from funeral supermarkets, and some funeral directors are willing to supply them. Biodegradable cardboard coffins are now commonplace, and can be obtained from numerous sources starting at about £60 plus delivery: the Natural Death Centre★ can give advice. The cheaper forms of cardboard coffin have their limitations regarding both strength and appearance, although they have improved greatly in both respects in the last few years. Wickerwork, woven bamboo and willow coffins are also now readily available, and the cost should be comparable with veneered chipboard coffins.

Waiting for the funeral

A decision must be made as to where the coffined body is to be stored until the funeral takes place. This will usually be a room of the house, which will need to be kept as cool as possible. Ensure that all heating is turned off, and that there is constant ventilation. Some diseases and/or types of drug treatment cause bodily decomposition to begin far more quickly than normal: it may be necessary to arrange for the body to be embalmed, especially in summer. Portable air-conditioners may be hired from an equipment-hire company to help keep the temperature low.

If the deceased died in hospital, it may be possible for the body to remain in the hospital mortuary until the day before the funeral.

Funeral transport

The coffin can be taken to the funeral in the back of a large estate car, Land Rover or horse and carriage. Hearses and horse-drawn hearses can be hired if preferred. It is unwise for bearers to carry the coffin any further than is strictly necessary.

Burial on your own property

It is possible to arrange for a burial to take place on your own land, in a garden, field or woodland. You must advise the environmental health officer of your intentions, as restrictions may apply if the local water table is likely to be affected (see pages 95–6). If such a private burial is being considered, it should be discussed with the local authorities some time before death is expected to take place.

There are other potential difficulties to be considered. Should the relatives of the deceased decide for any reason to move house, the presence of a grave on the property may present problems. The emotional decision to leave the grave behind must be faced, as must the fact that its presence will mean that the selling price of the house will almost certainly drop – possibly by 25 to 50 per cent. If the family wants to take the body to a new location, a Home Office licence for exhumation will be required: to move the body without this is a criminal offence.

Application for exhumation must be made on forms which the Home Office★ will supply; there is now no charge for this licence, but the process of exhumation will almost certainly involve professional assistance, be expensive and involve practical and psychological difficulties.

Unless a small part of private grounds can be set aside in perpetuity as a private cemetery, which may well be possible on an estate, farm or family house with a large garden, arrangements for burial at home are likely to present difficulties. A reasonable solution to this problem is to arrange for a cremation, and then to scatter or bury the ashes in the garden or field. Technically, an ashes casket buried in private ground is subject to the same laws of exhumation as a coffin; it can, however, legally be moved from one part of the private grounds to another. If ashes caskets are 'buried' *above* ground in, say, a purpose-built rockery or mausoleum, the casket can be moved elsewhere without difficulty.

Funeral management schemes

Many funeral directors are eager to see their clients more involved in funeral arrangements, being aware that this will assist with the grieving process. Some offer a service to clients who want to arrange funerals for their relatives themselves, and are prepared to sell them a coffin at a reasonable price, hire out a hearse if so required and provide a management service for a set fee. The service would provide all the necessary documentation, with advice on how and where to make the necessary arrangements.

If, however, a client decides to pay a management fee, buy a coffin, hire a hearse and then pay the funeral director or hospital mortuary to prepare the body for a funeral, rent chapel of rest facilities and so on, the overall cost could possibly approach the cost of a funeral director's basic funeral. However, this is an unlikely scenario: most of those who want to arrange a funeral without a funeral director do so because they want to do as much as possible themselves.

Helpful advice on organising a funeral yourself can be obtained from the Natural Death Centre*. The centre also publishes the *Natural Death Handbook*, which gives advice and information on all aspects of arranging and conducting funerals yourself. This can be obtained from the centre at a cost of £14.99 including postage and packing, or £15.50 if paying by credit card.

Chapter 16

After the funeral

When the funeral service has finished, family and friends often gather for light refreshments at the house of the deceased, at the house of another member of the family, or at a local public house or restaurant. If required to do so, the funeral director will book catering at a local public venue, or arrange for caterers to come into the house during the funeral and provide for guests. Mourners need to be clearly informed about what has been arranged, and where they are to go.

Paying for the funeral

The funeral director will submit an account fairly soon after the funeral, and will appreciate payment as soon as possible: he or she has already paid out quite substantial sums for various services to enable the funeral to take place – but will, of course, understand if the account cannot be settled until a grant of probate or letters of administration have been issued (you must make this clear). All the major banks will release funds from frozen accounts to enable the funeral bill to be paid, if provided with a suitable funeral account from the funeral director, together with an original copy of the death certificate. Legally, payment of the funeral bill is the first claim on the estate of the deceased, taking priority over income tax and any other claims.

The funeral director's account should be as detailed as possible, showing separately what has been paid out to doctors, crematoria, ministers and so on, on your behalf, and what is due to his or her company as the fee for professional services rendered. This will enable you to verify that only authorised payments have been made.

Any gratuities given to mortuary or cemetery staff by the funeral director are normally considered as part of the inclusive charge; any tips to bearers or others officiating at the funeral would be at the discretion of the client.

All the payments that the funeral director will have made on behalf of the client should be expenses that would inevitably have been incurred; in addition to the necessities, he or she may have been asked to provide flowers, place obituary notices in newspapers, provide catering and service sheets, and so on.

The services of the funeral director, minister and cemetery or crematorium are exempt from VAT. If, however, the funeral director supplies flowers, catering, printed service sheets or any form of memorial, the VAT must be paid on these items.

Memorials

Relatives often want to place a memorial tablet or headstone in a churchyard or cemetery where a coffin or ashes casket has been buried. Both churchyards and municipal cemeteries impose restrictions on the size and type of memorial and on the kind of stone that may be used and the type of lettering inscribed on it. Many cemeteries and almost all churchyards currently prohibit kerbs or surrounds to graves, and memorials are often restricted to a headstone or a plinth and vase set at the head of the grave.

Churchyard memorials

The rules applying to memorials in churchyards are generally more restrictive than in municipal or private cemeteries. Normally each diocese publishes guidelines for memorialisation, and incumbents are increasingly coming under pressure to enforce compliance. Usually, there are limitations as to the size of the memorial, the type of stone and the wording of the inscription. The general rule is that the type of stone used in the memorial must conform to the stone used in the building of the church; thus churches built of Portland stone (or similar) will often restrict memorial stones to either Portland or Purbeck, and will not allow granite or marble; 'flint' churches, on the other hand, will often require granite or similar materials in order to conform to the appearance of the church.

Quite apart from the size limitations imposed by the Archbishops' Council, most churchyards have a maximum permissible size for stone tablets marking the spot where cremated remains (ashes) have been buried; sometimes these are as small as 230mm × 230mm, with only a name and date of death allowed as inscriptions. The rules will vary according to traditional practice or the preference of the vicar.

Neither reserving a grave in a churchyard by faculty, where this is still possible (see page 93), nor purchasing the exclusive right of burial in a cemetery, automatically provides the right to put up any kind of memorial. For this, approval must be gained from the respective authorities and a fee paid.

In the Parochial Fees Order, the Archbishops' Council lays down the charges for the placement of memorials in the churchyards of the Church of England.

Fees in 2005 are as follows:

- small wooden cross — £16
- vase (not exceeding 305mm × 203mm × 203mm) — £67
- tablet for cremated remains (up to 450mm × 300mm) — £67
- any other memorial, including inscription — £131
- additional inscription, added later — £30

Anything other than a simple headstone or inscription requires the granting of a faculty, as does any unusual wording. The wording of an inscription must be approved by the incumbent. Many object to colloquialism and informal descriptions, and will generally stipulate that any quotations are either biblical or otherwise religious. The incumbent will advise on how to apply for a faculty, and a fee will be charged for this. It should be noted that a change of incumbent in a parish church may result in a different interpretation of guidelines, and local regulations may be relaxed or tightened accordingly. What was allowed before may not be allowed now.

Memorials in cemeteries

Municipal and private cemeteries are generally less rigorous in legislating about types of stone and the wording of inscriptions than churchyards but many authorities, faced with increasing difficulties of maintenance, insist that only 'lawn' graves with a simple headstone will be permitted. It is important to check out what limitations are imposed on memorials by the cemetery before a burial takes place, although this may be the last thing in mind when arranging a funeral.

The funeral director is frequently involved in these arrangements, and will warn clients of any restrictions he or she knows about; it is important to tell the funeral director of the family's probable intentions regarding a memorial as soon as possible. Some funeral directors provide their own service of memorial masonry; almost all have contact with stonemasons whom they use as subcontractors. Again, it must be remembered that a fee will be charged by the burial authorities for putting a memorial in place, in addition to the charge for the exclusive right of burial and the interment fee.

Memorials at crematoria

About a week after a cremation has taken place, the crematorium will usually send a brochure to the next of kin explaining what kinds of memorials are available. These are all optional, are not covered by the fees paid for cremation, and are subject to the payment of VAT.

The most popular means of memorial at the crematorium is the 'Book of Remembrance'. Hand-lettered inscriptions in the book usually consist of the name, date of death, and a short epitaph; the charge depends on the length of the entry. The crematorium displays the book, open at the right page, on the anniversary of death or of the funeral: the relatives choose which they prefer. Some crematoria sell a miniature reproduction of the entry in the form of a card, or bound as a booklet, the price of which depends on the quality of the presentation.

Charges for the erection of memorial plaques or for inscriptions on panels in memorial passages, where available, vary greatly. Some municipal crematoria will allow no memorial other than the entry in the Book of Remembrance.

Some crematoria have a colonnade of niches for ashes called a columbarium; the ashes are either walled in by a plaque or left in an urn in the niche. Most of these are now full, and where there are spaces charges are high. Some new, private crematoria, however, have recently made extensive provision for these and other similar memorials.

Other crematoria have memorial trees, or rose bushes; these are usually arranged in beds, where the memorial bush is chosen by the family, the ashes scattered around it, and a small plaque placed nearby. Costs vary, as does the length of time for which the crematorium will provide maintenance before another charge is made.

Bereaved families should beware of 'cold calling' memorial salespeople, who search the local papers for bereavement notices and attempt to make doorstep sales.

Arranging for a memorial

The funeral director or monumental mason will normally apply to the church or cemetery authorities for permission to erect a memorial; a copy of the entry in the burial register or the deeds of the grave may be required before authority is given.

After a burial, several months should be allowed for settlement before any memorial is erected or replaced. Time should be taken in the consideration and purchase of a memorial; unsolicited memorial salespeople should be ignored. Names of established local firms of monumental masons can be obtained from the National Association of Memorial Masons★ or the Association of Burial Authorities★.

Do not, under any circumstances, order a memorial from any source before ascertaining what the burial ground regulations are.

The cost of memorials varies enormously, depending on the type of stone, size, ornamentation, finish and lettering. Before ordering a memorial, ask for a written estimate which states clearly the items and total cost, including any delivery or erection charges and cemetery fees. It is normal for the stonemason to ask for a 50 per cent deposit to be paid by the client on confirmation of the order: this may seem a lot, but if the client changes his or her mind, there is not much the mason can do with the already inscribed stone.

VAT is charged on the provision of a new headstone or on adding a new inscription to an old one; it is not levied on the removal and replacement of existing memorials. The cemetery fee for the erection of a memorial is also exempt from VAT.

Memorials online

With the rapid increase in the number of people who now have access to the Internet and email has come the development of an

Internet memorial business. In addition to websites giving information about grief support services, there are sites which will help you to develop your own web page. While these sites will only last as long as the relevant webmaster is in business – and some sites have come and gone since the last edition of this book – they provide the opportunity for posting a much fuller obituary than is possible in national or local papers, and at considerably less cost. Websites may include photographs, video clips and music; for an example of the type of service available, check out *www.in-memoriam-uk.com* or *www.foreveronline.org*. When checking for relevant sites on the Internet, be sure to set your search pattern to UK sites only, or you will be inundated with details of US sites, many of which are good, but not related to the situation in the UK.

An increasing number of UK-based sites provide not only memorials but also information about funerals and bereavement; for example, a regional list of all the funeral directors in England and Wales can be found at *www.uk-funerals.co.uk*. This site can give information about your nearest funeral director, and provide much helpful detail. If more stylish or unusual funerals are contemplated, *www.lifewithoutyou.co.uk* offers a considerable amount of information and advice. Those looking for details of green funerals may find *www.peacefunerals.co.uk* useful, and an interesting site for those with a preference for two wheels rather than four is *www.motorcycle-funerals.com*.

Any fees can usually be paid by postal cheque to the UK sites, or online by credit card. Buying online is generally safe but users should take precautions. Look for secure websites (usually marked as such) and keep a record of emails and other transactions, or use traditional methods such as phone, fax or post to avoid giving your credit-card details electronically. Note that sites may change their content and locations frequently, and information may be inaccurate.

Charitable donations

An increasing amount of people ask family and friends to make donations to a nominated charity in memory of the deceased, and regard this as a fitting memorial for the person concerned. Usually, the funeral director will collect and forward donations to the appropriate charity, sending receipts to each donor and providing the charity and family with a list of donations received. The funeral director will not normally charge for this service.

Dealing with unwanted mail

The considerable amount of junk mail that is merely annoying for most people can become extremely painful when unwanted mail addressed to the person who has just died continues to arrive. The Mailing Preference Service (MPS)★ will stop most direct junk mail, while the Bereavement Register★ has been specifically designed to stop mail arriving for someone who has just died. Both services warn that some delay of a few weeks should be expected before the amount of unwanted mail diminishes, as many companies that send out junk mail update their databases only every few weeks.

Chapter 17

Death away from home

As people move from place to place more often nowadays, they often express a wish to be buried or cremated in a district other than the one in which they died. In such cases, funeral arrangements have to be made in two places: where the death occurred, and where the funeral is to take place. Most funeral directors are accustomed to this, but if the distance involved is too great, the funeral director may subcontract arrangements at the other end to a colleague on the spot.

Bodies are usually conveyed by hearse within the UK, as this is normally the quickest and cheapest form of transport. It is quite possible to send a coffin by rail or air, but this is likely to be more expensive: the coffin must be suitably packaged and covered with hessian, and for air transport, taken to the carrier's cargo department at the airport four hours before despatch. Charges vary according to the distance and route covered, but airlines may charge a special rate for carrying a coffin with a body inside.

The packaged coffin must be accompanied by all the necessary documents for the funeral, and the body must normally be embalmed if it is to be conveyed by any form of public transport. It is also normal practice to ensure that a body is embalmed before carrying it any considerable distance by hearse. Most funeral directors will deal with a distant funeral by accompanying the hearse and driver, and hiring bearers at the other end from a local colleague.

Registration must be effected in the registration district where the person died, and not where the funeral is to take place; it is, however, possible to give the information to a registrar in the funeral location, subject to the conditions in Chapter 3, 'Registering the death'.

Death abroad

When a British subject dies abroad, whether as a resident or as a visitor, the death must be registered where he or she died according to local regulations and customs. This is far from uncommon: in recent years, more than 2,000 British deaths abroad have been reported annually to the Foreign Office. In many countries, the British consul can also register the death: this has the advantage that certified copies of the entry in the Register of Deaths can eventually be obtained from the General Register Office*, just as if the death had been registered in the UK.

If it is required that the death be recorded in the consular register in order to make records of the death available in the UK, the next of kin or executor should obtain, complete and return an application form to the Nationality and Passport Section of the Foreign and Commonwealth Office (FCO)*, together with the death certificate issued by the local authorities in the country concerned. If the consular office in the country where the death occurred is aware of the death, a separate document bearing a consular stamp is usually included with the package of documents accompanying the body. This document should also be sent to the Nationality and Passport Section of the FCO with the application form. If the consular office where the death took place is not aware of the death, then the passport and birth certificate should be sent with the application as proof of UK citizenship; these will be returned to the applicant.

A consular fee is payable for the registration of the death in the UK, and a further fee is payable for each certificate issued at the time of registration; these fees vary periodically, and applicants should ask the FCO what fees are needed to accompany their application. This is a lengthy process, and considerable delay should be expected.

If such application is not made, there will be no official record of the death in the UK. In this case, in order for the funeral to take place the registrar of the relevant district must be asked to supply a registrar's certificate confirming that the death is not required to be registered, commonly called a 'certificate of no liability to register'. For this, a copy of the foreign death certificate, suitably translated into English (although many European countries now use a multi-lingual death certificate which does not need translation), must be supplied, giving the cause of death. The funeral director will normally be able to obtain both the translation and the certificate. Consular registration can take place after the funeral: a 'certificate of no liability to register' does not inhibit this process.

If someone dies while abroad, and their identity cannot be fully established after extensive investigation, the local officials will complete a death certificate with as much detail as they know, and eventually provide a funeral in accordance with the custom of the country where the death occurred.

Death at sea

When a death occurs on a foreign ship, it counts as a death abroad; the death must be recorded in the ship's log, and the port superintendent where the ship's crew are discharged must make enquiries into the cause of death.

When death occurs on a British-registered ship, the death is recorded in the captain's log, and all facts and particulars relating to the death must be recorded and delivered to the Registry of Shipping and Seamen* on arrival at any port within or outside the UK. The master of any ship has the authority to decide whether, for health reasons, a body should be immediately disposed of at sea, or kept for disposal later. As in most of these cases the death is unexpected, the body is usually kept in order to assist with a coroner's enquiry. Most cruise ships have mortuary facilities for cold storage of those who have died on board.

When a body is brought into a British port, the death must be reported to the coroner in whose jurisdiction the port is located. He or she may decide to order an enquiry, in which case the body cannot be moved without his or her consent. The registrar of the district in which the funeral is to take place must also issue a 'certificate of no liability to register', for which either a copy of the entry in the captain's log or a death certificate must be obtained. Copies of log entries can be obtained from the shipping company which owns the ship concerned, or the port superintendent where the body was brought ashore. Copies of the death certificate may be obtained from the Registry of Shipping and Seamen. This will normally all be dealt with by the funeral director.

Death in the air

When death occurs in an aircraft, the death must be registered in the country to which that aircraft belongs. At the next landing following the death, the captain must notify the local police authorities and the appropriate registration authority, which may not be in the same country as the one where the aircraft has landed. Subsequent action concerning arrangements for the body varies according to local regulations, but as far as relatives are concerned the procedure is the same as that for a death which occurs abroad. These arrangements can be extremely complicated, and will normally be dealt with by the funeral director in conjunction with a specialist repatriation service.

Returning a body from abroad

When someone dies abroad and the body is to be returned to the UK, the process is complex and expensive. Holiday or travel insurance which covers repatriation is essential, as the cost can run to several thousand pounds. Those who are travelling on package holidays should immediately contact their holiday representative: the biggest tour operators have proper procedures for handling bereavement. Further, tour operators belonging to ABTA subscribe to a code of conduct which commits them to assistance in many areas of bereavement, even where death occurs from an activity outside the normal holiday arrangements. They are also able to provide help with legal costs where necessary. Those travelling independently should ensure that their insurance covers repatriation, and be aware of the emergency telephone number on which to contact the insurance company or travel agency. Note that normal holiday insurance does not usually cover dangerous sports such as paragliding or scuba diving; additional cover must be taken out to cover such activities.

The British consul in the area will be able to advise, but will not be able to help financially. The consul may be some distance from where death occurred: in the Caribbean or Greek islands he or she may well not be on the same island. Independent travellers should also contact the local police or ambulance service as soon as possible. If there appears to be no one to advise, it would be wise to telephone a reputable funeral director in the UK to ask for advice and assistance; most funeral directors are experienced in these matters, and can turn to specialist repatriation services if they need help.

If the deceased had no insurance and the high cost of repatriation cannot be met, local cremation may be the only option available; it will almost certainly be the cheapest option. Provided a certificate of contents is obtained from the crematorium, the ashes can be brought back to the UK as hand luggage. This option, however, is not always available: most Muslim countries have no facilities for cremation, while in Nepal bodies are normally cremated on open-air funeral pyres, which may be found unacceptable.

The death must be registered in the country and area concerned, and death certificates and the doctor's medical certificate of the cause of death obtained. The local judicial authorities may want to investigate and, in any case, authority must be obtained from them to move the body out of their country. The body must be embalmed before it can be moved, and a certificate of embalming will be required. The body must be contained in a metal-lined coffin, which in turn must be suitably packaged and covered with hessian. All necessary papers for customs clearance must be obtained and accompany the coffin, and arrangements should be made with an airline to convey the body to the UK – the usual method of repatriation.

Insurance companies will have contracts with repatriation services or firms of international funeral directors who will attend to all of this; if there is no insurance it is possible for relatives to attend to the matter, but specialist knowledge and a great deal of patience are required and the matter would be better entrusted to a UK funeral director. On arrival in the UK, customs clearance must be obtained; this may take several hours, but, once cleared, the body must be removed from the airport as soon as possible.

If death has occurred due to natural causes, the coroner will have only minimal involvement. If death is not due to natural causes, but is the result of an accident or criminal activity, the coroner in whose jurisdiction the airport lies will want to hold an inquest, and the body may not be moved from the mortuary until permission is given.

The registrar of the district in which the funeral is to take place must be informed, so that a 'certificate of no liability to register' can be issued. For this, evidence of death and the cause of death will be required.

Funerals involving burial

If the funeral is to involve burial, all the documents received with the coffin must be taken to the registrar in the district where the funeral will take place, with the relevant papers suitably translated. The funeral director will normally attend to this, or the coroner's office may be able to help. The registrar will issue a 'certificate of no liability to register', which takes the place of the green certificate (see page 30) and is the only document required by burial authorities, whether a church or local authority.

Funerals involving cremation

If the funeral is to involve cremation, the local registrar must issue a 'certificate of no liability to register' as in the case of burial, but considerable further paperwork is involved. Application must be made to the Home Office★ for authority to cremate; a certificate will be issued which will take the place of statutory **Forms B** and **C**. To obtain this, statutory **Form A** must be completed and signed, and taken to the Home Office with all the documents received from abroad with the coffin. These should include an original document (or certified copy of an original document) that gives a specific cause of death. This does not necessarily have to be a death certificate: it may be a consular death certificate, a doctor's certificate or a mortuary certificate. If originals or certified copies of the relevant documents do not accompany the returned coffin, the funeral directors that assisted with the deceased in the country where he or she died – or whoever issued the original documents – should be contacted so that a certified copy can be requested. In certain circumstances the Consular Division of the Foreign and Commonwealth Office (FCO)★ may be able to help. If documents are in a foreign language, it is the responsibility of the applicant to have them officially translated. However, some European countries now use a multi-lingual death certificate, with each relevant section in five languages. In most cases, the Home Office will usually be willing to accept documents in most Western European languages: if there is any doubt, the Office should be contacted in advance.

Obviously this will be time-consuming, and plans for the funeral must be adjusted accordingly. If sent by post, the envelope containing the papers should be marked 'Cremation papers:

Urgent'; it will be quicker to take the papers personally and wait while they are processed. Sometimes the specialist company that arranged for the repatriation is able to do this on the client's behalf, but normally the funeral director will attend to this.

Counter service at the Home Office is currently available from Monday to Friday between the hours of 11am and 12.30pm, and 2.30pm and 4pm; processing should take about 20 minutes.

All documents received from or returned by the Home Office should then be taken to the local registrar in order to obtain a 'certificate of no liability to register'; all these papers must then be submitted to the crematorium, although other than the certificate of no liability most documents (including any copies of foreign death certificates) will be returned.

In some developing countries, the only form of death certificate issued is a carbon-copy or photocopy of the written entry in the local register of deaths. Unless this is supplied as a certified copy, it is likely to present a problem to UK registrars, whose rules require them to see an original document; however, if documents are acceptable to the Home Office they should also be acceptable to the registrar.

When the coroner is involved

Repatriations invariably involve returning the body to the UK by air. If death appears to have been caused by something other than natural causes, the coroner of the district where the funeral is to take place must be informed. He or she may order a post mortem and, if this satisfies the coroner that death did occur from natural causes, the necessary documents will be issued from the coroner's office. If the funeral involves burial, the coroner will authorise a 'certificate of no liability to register', which is all that will be required; if it involves cremation, he or she will issue the coroner's certificate for cremation, and the Home Office will not be involved at all.

If, after consultation, the coroner declines jurisdiction because he or she is satisfied without carrying out a post mortem that death was due to natural causes, the Home Office will consider the application on receipt of confirmation of the coroner's decision.

If the coroner finds that death was not due to natural causes, he or she will order an inquest to be held, the results of which may well be inconclusive due to the embalming or deterioration of the body and the inability to call witnesses. In such a case, the funeral cannot be held until authority to do so is received from the coroner.

Sending a body abroad

When someone who has died in England or Wales is going to be buried or cremated in another country (including Scotland, Northern Ireland and the Channel Islands), permission must first be obtained from the local coroner. **Form 104** gives notice to a coroner of the intention to remove a body from England, which will be supplied by the registrar or funeral director: usually the funeral director deals with this.

If the registrar knows before registration that the body is to be taken out of England, he or she will not issue a certificate for burial or cremation; if, however, such a certificate has already been issued, it must be sent to the coroner together with the 'out of England' form. Four clear working days must normally elapse before the coroner gives permission on **Form 103**. However, in cases of urgency, a personal visit to the coroner's office with all necessary documentation and information concerning the death will, provided the coroner is satisfied, enable the form to be signed and the body removed immediately. If the coroner is investigating the death, he or she will not release the body for removal from England until satisfied that it will not be required for further examination.

There are no legal restrictions on taking cremated remains out of the UK, but other countries may impose their own restrictions. For example, Italy is the most difficult: the ashes are treated exactly the same as a body, with all the same documents required, together with permission to import from the local prefect of police in the area of intended disposal. A hermetically sealed container is required, the sealing of which must have been witnessed by a representative of the consul. Greece treats ashes in the same way as an exhumed body, which may not be imported into the country until one year after death. France requires consular sealing of a hermetically sealed container bearing an engraved plate which gives the name of the deceased, date of death and death certificate number. India requires a High Commission permit. Always check specifications with the relevant embassy or consulate.

Making the arrangements

Making the arrangements to take a body into another country for burial or cremation is usually an extremely complex matter and should not be contemplated without expert help and advice. Generally, the body must be embalmed and contained in a metal-lined coffin which must be suitably packaged. All necessary freight documents must be completed, and a death certificate provided for UK customs clearance. Consular requirements of the destination country must be met, and all documents required must be translated and authenticated at the relevant consulate for a fee.

Consular regulations

Consular regulations change frequently, so in every case enquiries should be made at the local consulate of the country concerned.

The requirements usually include:

- consular permission to take the body into the relevant country
- a copy of the certificate of death supplied by the registrar, suitably translated
- an official certificate stating the cause of death and a declaration that sanitary regulations for transporting the body will be met
- a certificate of embalming
- a declaration from the funeral director that the coffin contains only the body of the deceased and accompanying clothing and packing
- details of the route, flight number and date of departure
- a 'freedom from infection' (FFI) certificate
- a certificate of exhumation and a copy of the Home Office licence to exhume, in the case of exhumed bodies
- a passport wherever it is necessary for the body to pass through another country on the way to its destination – this does not apply to air transport
- a consul representative's presence at the sealing of the coffin/crate.

In addition, the consulate will also provide information about formalities that will be required on arrival of the body, and what arrangements must be made beforehand.

Burial at sea

Burial at sea may be requested by anyone; it is relatively unusual, fairly complicated and very expensive. All materials disposed of at sea require a licence under the Food and Environmental Protection Act 1985 · (modified by the Environmental Protection Act 1990); this includes bodies, but in order to minimise stress to the bereaved, the government will, in place of issuing a licence, accept written notification from a funeral director that he or she intends to bury a body at sea.

The letter must contain the name and address of the applicant (normally the funeral director), the date and time period for which permission is required, and the information that a human body is to be disposed of at sea. This should be sent to the Sea Fisheries Inspectorate★, or the local Fisheries District Inspector at the Needles, Isle of Wight or at Newhaven, East Sussex – these are the only two coastal locations where sea burials are currently allowed.

Time must be allowed for a reply, and other documentation must be gathered. Registration must take place in the district where death occurred, although information may be given at any register office (see Chapter 3). An application must be made to the coroner on **Form 104** to remove the body from the English mainland; the coroner will give permission for the body to be removed and buried at sea on **Form 103**. A copy of the death certificate will also be required, together with a 'Freedom From Infection' certificate stating that death was not caused by an infectious disease.

The Sea Fisheries Inspectorate will give advice on obtaining permission from the Fisheries District Inspector, which will give permission only for the two specified locations. The coffin must be made from solid wood, have many holes drilled in it, and contain suitable heavy weights to ensure that it will sink. Where such burials are preceded by a church service, the coffin should be covered with a pall to cover the holes.

Arrangements for a suitable vessel must be made, allowing for the fact that not only must a heavy coffin be carried and lowered into the sea in a respectful way, but also that a number of passengers will want to accompany it on the boat. Local harbourmasters can be a source of relevant information; generally, however, all such arrangements can be made by an experienced funeral director. A specialist company dealing with sea burials is Britannia Shipping Company for Burial at Sea Ltd★.

No documents are required for scattering or burying ashes at sea.

Death while in the armed forces

If a member of the forces dies serving abroad, the Ministry of Defence (MOD) normally allows the next of kin the choice of:

- **a funeral overseas** with two people from the UK (normally the next of kin) attending, all at public expense; or
- **repatriation of the body** where practicable at public expense to a funeral director in the UK chosen by the family. Once the body has reached the funeral director, the family becomes responsible for the funeral. The MOD provides the coffin and a grant of up to £1,309 towards burial, or up to £798 towards cremation.

If a serviceman or servicewoman dies in the UK, the next of kin have the following choices:

- **a military funeral at public expense** This will be arranged and paid for by the MOD, provided it takes place near to where the death occurred. (Exceptionally, because military funerals cannot normally be arranged in Northern Ireland, a member of the forces dying there can be buried anywhere in the UK)
- **a private funeral with limited military assistance** The MOD pays for the coffin and conveyance of the body from the place of death to a funeral director chosen by the family. Once the body has reached the funeral director's premises, the family becomes responsible for the rest of the funeral arrangements. The MOD will pay a grant of up to £1,309 towards the cost of burial, and up to £798 in the case of cremation
- **a private-expense funeral** In this case, the next of kin arrange for the body to be collected and make all the necessary arrangements for the funeral privately. The MOD will give up to £1,500 towards the cost of burial, and up to £958 for cremation.

A member of the forces who dies while serving may be buried in a military cemetery by consultation with the appropriate cemetery authorities. This will be arranged at public expense if there is a military cemetery near to where the death occurred.

If someone who was receiving a war disablement pension dies as a result of that disablement or was drawing a constant attendance allowance, the Department for Work and Pensions (DWP)★ may pay for a simple funeral. The next of kin should contact the Veterans Agency★ straight away, before any formal arrangements are made.

Chapter 18

The grief process

Death alters the course of daily life for all those closest to the person who has died. If someone close to you has died, you must accept that things will change, whether the change is small or immense. Something irreversible has happened and your life must now follow a different course. You will face various experiences which will affect you in certain ways until, having worked through them, you arrive at a point where your life is once again moving steadily in a positive direction.

Normal grief

Bereavement is a very complex issue; this short chapter describes many of the phases that you may encounter when recently bereaved. Any description of reactions to grief has to be simplified because of the enormous variation from person to person in coping with the situation. Nevertheless, the considerable amount of study which has taken place over the last 25 years has revealed much that is common to the great majority of people.

There is nothing unusual about grieving: it is 'normal' and most people will make a 'normal' recovery without a great deal of assistance. Some, however, get stuck somewhere in the process of recovery and need help; others (fortunately, only a few) are so affected by their bereavement that the grief process gets out of hand. In such cases, treatment as well as assistance is needed, counsel as well as care. The normal grief processes only are covered in this section to help you understand how you may be feeling.

Most of the time, bereavement causes a great deal of pain; many people do not acknowledge this, fearing that they will be marked out as weak and abnormal. Family and friends will often avoid people who have lost partners, children or close friends, usually because they are embarrassed and do not know what to say. They excuse their feelings of embarrassment and helplessness by saying things like: 'Grief is a very private affair. I don't want to intrude.' So the bereaved are often deserted just when they need most support, which leads them to believe that it is their pain and tears that cause others to shun them; they therefore make determined efforts to 'be strong' and suppress their natural emotional responses. More than anything else, this hinders recovery from grief.

Reactions to grief

When loss has occurred and the bereaved person has been diverted from the accustomed course of life, a number of psychological forces come into effect. The different stages of grief that a person may go through include shock, sorrow, anger, apathy and depression, before the process of recovery can begin. Not everyone experiences all of these emotions, and some stages may last longer than others. In other words, everyone is different.

Shock: the primary experience
The initial effect of bereavement is shock. There is a numbness in which the rest of the world often seems to recede, leaving the bereaved person in mental limbo; a common feeling is of the world carrying on but the person no longer feeling part of it. This leads almost immediately into a stage of denial – the strong feeling that death cannot possibly have occurred, that the bereaved is dreaming, that the doctors have made a mistake. This begins at the moment of loss and has its major impact during the first two to three days. At this stage, people can be very susceptible; this should be recognised and great care taken when an important decision has to be made – especially the arrangements for the funeral. Dates and times often have to be decided upon quickly, but sufficient time should be allowed before the funeral to avoid making the wrong decisions in haste.

When death occurs after a long illness, or where there was ill-feeling between the deceased and the bereaved, the initial response is a feeling of relief: the tension is at last over and done with. This may be accompanied almost at once by a sense of guilt for feeling relieved – talking about this to a sensible and trustworthy friend will help.

Sorrow: the underlying experience

Shock often overlaps with or is followed by feelings of sorrow – the sadness which develops as the person becomes aware that an irreversible loss has occurred. Sorrow and pining can have the effects of physical pain, often made worse by the belief that one is supposed to 'be strong' and not show any undue signs of emotional disturbance. At this point, the bereaved person needs to be free to express grief with the support of others who will not be embarrassed or try to suppress the person's tears. In order to make a good recovery, the bereaved person needs to feel this pain, express it and work through it in ways which are appropriate to his or her personality.

But initial sorrow is often accompanied by unreasonable guilt. People often feel guilty because they think they could have done more than they did – had they done more, perhaps the deceased person would not have died – and much reassurance and patience are called for. This often leads to people 'bargaining' with God or with life in general (for example, by promising to be good if only they can wake up to find that it was all a bad dream). The only way to help someone going through these emotions is to root the person firmly in reality, to talk about the death and to have the person visit the body in a chapel of rest, thus allowing a gradual acceptance of the situation to come about in a way that can be coped with.

The acute stage of this phase does not usually last for very long and is sometimes over in two or three weeks. The sorrow will persist but will generally subside into a numbing ache. The guilt (real or imagined) may well last for a long time.

Anger: the developing experience

Many people get very angry when bereaved, usually in an irrational manner. There is anger with God (for letting death happen), with friends and family (for not understanding or for not being bereaved themselves), with themselves (for not coping) and with the deceased (for having died and left them). Sometimes the anger comes before the sorrow and guilt, sometimes after, and is often compounded by a strong and irrational resentment and a certain amount of aggression (depending on the person's personality – a very mild person is unlikely to become extremely aggressive). Friends need a great deal of patience: they should let the person cool down, then listen to the anger without being defensive or argumentative.

This stage of the grief process can last from a few days to several months. It may continue to simmer in the background for a long time, resulting in outbursts of irrational anger at unexpected times. Those on the receiving end should remember that the anger is not directed at them and should try not to feel injured or aggrieved.

Apathy and depression

When the anger calms down, a state of apathy often develops. The bereaved person displays indifference to what is going on round about him or her and may show a considerable reluctance to make decisions. Patience and encouragement are needed continuously.

Or there may be feelings of depression. Most people can work through these normal feelings of depression with the support of friends and family; however, this support should not be allowed to turn into an unhealthy dependence on the help of others – it is important to encourage people by doing things *with* them rather than *for* them, so that they will once again be able to do things for themselves. Occasionally, depression can degenerate into acute depression, where professional assistance is called for.

Recovery

Gradually, even when the pain of bereavement has been acute, a sense of acceptance grows and the bereaved person once again begins to take an interest in life. When it becomes possible for the person to make positive plans for the future and again find pleasure in everyday experience, the bereaved person is well on the way to recovery. Life will never be the same again, but it can now be lived in a normal, healthy manner.

Other common reactions

Shock can also have physical effects, leading to quite genuine symptoms. These are often not recognised as being part of the normal grief process and, as a result, many recently bereaved people worry that they have a physical illness on top of the burden of bereavement.

Headaches are common, as are a continuously dry mouth, weakness, breathlessness, oversensitivity to noise, tightness in the chest and throat, a hollow feeling in the stomach, giddiness and nausea. Hair loss may also occur. Some people lose weight, others put it on; some people are constantly tired, even when they have had sufficient sleep and food.

There are often real feelings of fear, sometimes based on the person's anxiety that he or she will not be able to cope. Absentmindedness and lack of ability to concentrate on anything for very long are also common: sometimes people forget what they were saying in mid-sentence. Memory is frequently affected: facts, names, experiences, all well known, cannot be brought to mind when needed, which can be very upsetting.

All of these are quite normal experiences and recognising them as such will greatly assist you to live through them and come to terms with the reality of the bereavement which has occurred.

On the way to recovery

In practice, of course, it is seldom as simple as this. Some people do not appear to go through any of the emotional phases listed above, while others pass from feeling to feeling, only to repeat the process a few weeks later. Realising that there is no one certain way that you're *supposed* to feel will help you on your way to recovery.

Chapter 19

Child and cot deaths

Every year, many babies are stillborn, or die within the first month of life; approximately one couple in 500 has suffered this form of bereavement. Yet only in recent years has this experience been recognised as real bereavement, especially in the case of children who were stillborn; previously parents who had lost newborn babies were expected to recover quickly from their losses.

Research indicates that mourning often lasts longer among bereaved parents than in widows and widowers; a survey of parents who had lost babies in the first few months of life indicated that two-thirds of those interviewed felt that their main need was to have their baby recognised as a real person, not just as 'something that could be replaced'.

Cot deaths

Cot death is the sudden and unexpected death of a baby for no obvious reason, although a post mortem examination may explain some occurrences of cot deaths. Those that remain unexplained after a post mortem examination may be registered as being caused by sudden infant death syndrome, or similar wording.

The majority of cot deaths occur in babies under the age of one year. The Foundation for the Study of Infant Deaths (FSID)★ launched a campaign called 'Reduce the Risks of Cot Death' in 1991, which offers parents life-saving advice. Since then, the number of babies under one dying of cot death in England and Wales has fallen by 75 per cent, but it was still as high as 295 in 2003. Between 1999 and 2003, 61 per cent of sudden infant deaths occurred among boys, and 89 per cent occurred among babies aged under six months.

Cot death still remains the leading kind of death in babies over one month old, claiming more lives than meningitis, leukaemia, other forms of cancer, household and road traffic accidents. Between 1996 and 2002, approximately 50 per cent of cot deaths occurred while the babies were sharing a bed with a parent or parents, and the Foundation strongly urges parents not to do this.

Advice given by the Foundation includes:

- putting the baby to sleep on its back
- cutting smoking during pregnancy (both parents)
- preventing any smoking in the same place as the baby at all times
- not letting the baby get too hot
- always putting the baby to sleep in its own cot or carrycot, and siting this in the parents' bedroom for the first six months.

The Foundation has produced a colourful 16-page booklet called *BabyZone*, with cartoons, aimed at reducing the risk of cot deaths. It contains evidence-based advice on protecting babies from accidents and infections, and is available free of charge by calling the Foundation. Those unfortunate enough to have experienced the sudden death of a baby, or those involved in trying to help them, would find the Foundation Helpline★ beneficial.

Stillbirths

The legal definition of a stillbirth is a baby born dead after 24 weeks of pregnancy (this was changed from a baby born dead after 28 weeks in 1992). Until the mid-1970s, the general attitude among hospitals and midwives was that it was better for the parents to know as little as possible about the dead child, and many hospitals dealt with the disposal without the mother seeing her child. Some hospitals held contracts for the burial of stillborn children; these were often buried in common, unmarked graves, and sometimes little or no record was kept.

Understanding of grief and bereavement has changed considerably since that time, and stillborn children are afforded the same dignified treatment as a young baby who dies. Most funeral directors will make no charge for arranging the funeral of a stillborn child; such funerals are usually burials, as the process of cremation will result in no ashes being available for possible burial and memorialisation.

Information in the media about the retention and disposal of organs and tissue following the post mortem examinations of babies and children has also focused attention on the disposal of stillbirths 20 to 30 years ago. Some parents have been able to trace the location of their child's burial, and appropriate memorial services on the burial site have afforded some comfort. Hospital chaplains and local funeral directors will do their best to assist parents who have anxieties in such matters.

Miscarriage involving a non-viable foetus

If a miscarriage occurs before the 24th week of pregnancy, it is legally regarded as a non-viable foetus, and there is no liability as to registration. After 24 weeks, it is regarded as a stillbirth and must be registered as such. Many parents now consider a pregnancy which does not come to full term at whatever stage of gestation as resulting in a child to be mourned, and which deserves a dignified funeral. Most such sad experiences occur in hospital, and many hospitals, led by their chaplains and bereavement teams, regard all such issue as a baby, whatever the number of weeks between conception and delivery.

Some hospitals will offer grieving parents a simple cremation funeral service, possibly carried out by a funeral director contracted to the hospital, for which there may be no charge. Of course, the parents may choose to make arrangements themselves with a funeral director of their choice, in which case they will be responsible for any charges which may be incurred. Some parents may not wish to be involved in such a funeral service, in which case the hospital will arrange for respectful disposal, and later offer a service of blessing to the family concerned.

The Royal College of Nursing makes a strong case for all products of conception to be treated in such a respectful and dignified way, and parents who find themselves in such a bereft situation should discuss the matter immediately with the hospital chaplain, however difficult or painful this may be.

Memorials

Mourning involves memories and when a small baby dies, memories are few. Until very recently, it used to be felt that the less the parents knew about the dead baby, the less they would grieve; the mother was often sedated and the dead child whisked away before she or the father could see it. Relatives were advised to dispose of any potential reminders: baby clothes were removed, pram and cot disposed of and toys given away or carefully hidden. This deprived the parents of almost all the grounds of memory, thus making it almost impossible for them to find a degree of healing through mourning.

Active contact with the dead baby greatly helps to make it a real person to bereaved parents, and supplies at least some of the memories they need. Mothers are more often encouraged to hold their dead baby, and to wash and dress it. Photographs can provide memories and confirm the reality of a child's existence, thus providing a source of comfort. Expensive equipment is unnecessary: a simple photograph will do. A lock of hair can be kept, or a little down snipped from the baby's head and kept in a transparent envelope. Handprints or footprints can be taken with washable ink pads, and suitably mounted. A toy or two intended for the baby can be placed with him or her in the coffin.

The funeral

Parents who have lost babies or small children should be encouraged to resist the temptation to get the funeral over with as soon as possible. The funeral service is one of the few things which bereaved parents can arrange for their babies, and as much time and thought as possible should go into discussing the details. The Foundation for the Study of Infant Deaths (FSID)* publishes a leaflet, *Information for Parents Following the Unexpected Death of their Baby*, which contains lots of helpful advice. The funeral will cause pain, but this pain is a necessary part of the healing and recovery process.

Many, probably most, funeral directors will make no charge for arranging the funeral of a baby or small child; funeral arrangements, services of staff, use of the chapel of rest, an appropriate coffin and a hearse or estate car will normally be provided free. If elaborate funeral arrangements are requested, such as a solid wood coffin or cars for mourners, these will have to be paid for. Many hospitals now make provision for the reverent disposal of miscarriages or stillbirths, with a simple funeral service often taking place in the hospital chapel or local crematorium.

Most crematoria do not charge for the cremation of children under the age of one year: it should be noted that some crematoria are unable to provide cremated remains for disposal afterwards, as the cremation process is usually total, leaving no ashes for disposal.

Many cemeteries also make no charge for the burial of infants under one year, and fees for burial in churchyards are frequently waived. Headstones or other memorial stones will, however, be subject to the same fees as adults'.

Care agencies

A number of care agencies exist for the sole purpose of offering help and support to those who have lost babies and small children, and those who are trying to help parents come to terms with their loss. Compassionate Friends★ – whose valuable function is not always recognisable from its name – is one such society. The Foundation for the Study of Infant Deaths is another.

Chapter 20

Probate, pensions and property

Sorting out the practical affairs of a person who has died can appear to be a very bewildering task; certainly, there is usually a lot to do, but it if taken one step at a time it should be fairly straightforward.

Probate

When a person dies, somebody has to deal with his or her estate – the money, property and possessions left. Money that is owed to the deceased person must be collected, any debts paid, and the remainder of the estate distributed to those people entitled to it.

The term 'probate' means the issuing of a legal document to one or more people recognising that they are authorised to deal with the estate in this way. The Probate Registry must approve the will, and until this is done, none of the deceased's property should be sold, given away or disposed of.

Application must be made to the nearest probate court, which will in due course issue a 'grant of representation'. This will be in one of three forms:

- **probate** issued to one or more of the executors named in the deceased's will
- **letters of administration (with will)** issued when there is a will but no executor is named, the executors have died or moved abroad, or do not wish to be involved
- **letters of administration** issued when the deceased has not made a will, or the will is invalid.

The grant of probate will take several weeks; granting letters of administration will take longer. For further information on how to administer an estate, see *Wills and Probate*, available from Which? Books★.

Purpose of a grant

Organisations such as banks, building societies and insurance companies which hold money in the deceased's name need to know to whom that money should be paid; the grant of representation is proof that the person named in it may collect such money.

The estate left when a person dies must be passed on to the people named in his or her will; if there is no valid will it passes to the next of kin (see page 158). The distribution of the estate to the correct people is the responsibility of the executor – the person named in the grant. The grant proves to anyone wishing to see it that the person so named is authorised to deal with the estate.

When is a grant required?

Probate is not normally required if the value of the estate totals less than £5,000; the guidelines of the probate court also allow probate to be dispensed with for sums in excess of this if the settlement of the estate is straightforward. If there are disputes about the settlement of the estate, or possible future complications are foreseen, probate should be applied for.

A grant may not be needed when organisations, such as building societies or insurance companies, holding the deceased's money are willing to release it to the executors; some building societies do not require probate for sums up to about £15,000. Probate will not normally be needed when a house is held in joint names and it is clear that the house automatically will become the property of the surviving partner. However, probate will be required in order to sell or transfer any property held only in the name of the deceased.

A house or flat should not be advertised for sale too soon after the death of the owner, as a sale cannot be completed until probate has been granted. The date of issue of the grant of probate cannot be guaranteed to coincide with the final stages of any sale. For more information on how to obtain probate, contact the Probate and Inheritance Tax Helpline★ or visit *www.courtservice.gov.uk*.

Who is entitled to a grant of probate?

If there is a will with named executors, they should apply for probate. If there are no named executors, or the executors are unable or unwilling to be involved, then the next person named in the will to whom the deceased leaves his or her estate should be prepared to act as executor and apply for probate.

If the deceased had not made a valid will, then application for probate should normally be made by his or her next of kin in the following order of priority:

- husband or wife
- sons or daughters
- parents
- brothers or sisters, or, if deceased, their sons or daughters
- other relatives.

Before probate or letters of administration are granted, the deceased's executors must inform the bank which holds accounts in his or her name. The bank can then arrange to freeze accounts, cancel cheque books and any debit or credit cards. Most banks will generally release funds to pay the funeral account if presented with an invoice from a funeral director.

The Post Office, building societies and any other institutions where the deceased had an account must also be notified; any savings will temporarily be frozen. The Inland Revenue should also be informed of the death.

After the grant of probate or letters of administration is issued, the executor(s) must settle all debts, obtain payments of any life insurance policies, and transfer the ownership of any house, shares or other property the deceased may have had. The executor should also advertise for any creditors and allow two months for claims to be made. Failure to do this could make the executor liable to pay future creditors.

The Scottish equivalent of probate is confirmation, and the equivalent of letters of administration is the appointment of an executor-dative.

Pensions and tax

All pension books and allowance books of the deceased must be returned, to the local Social Security office, the Department for Work and Pensions (DWP)★, Jobcentre Plus or to the issuing office quoted in the payment book; notes of the pension and/or allowance numbers should be carefully kept. If there are any uncashed orders, they must not be cashed after death, even if signed. Any unpaid amounts should be claimed when the book is returned. Any outstanding pension or allowance payments must be specifically claimed by the executors: they will not be paid automatically.

To get any unpaid portions of a war pension, write to the Veterans Agency★ or phone the Veterans Agency Helpline to claim the amount due, quoting the pension number.

If the deceased had been an officer in one of the armed forces and a pension or allowance was being paid on the basis of war service, the next payment that comes will have to be returned, uncashed, to the issuing office. Send with it a note of the place and date of death, and claim any amount that has become due in the period from the last payment to the death.

If income tax was being deducted from the deceased's salary under the pay-as-you-earn (PAYE) scheme, a refund of tax may be due. Income received by the deceased will be taxed in the normal way up to the date of death; depending on the circumstances there may be some tax to be paid, or a repayment to be claimed. If you are the next of kin or executor, and are administering the estate of the person who died, you should notify the Inland Revenue office which dealt with his or her affairs as soon as possible. The Inland Revenue will then arrange any refund of tax due or to collect any tax owing from the estate. If you do not know which office it was, look for tax forms among the deceased's papers, or ask the former employer or pension payer. If this fails to produce the information, contact the nearest Inland Revenue office. You may find the Inland Revenue★ booklet IR45 *What to Do About Tax When Someone Dies* helpful. See also *www.inlandrevenue.gov.uk* for further details of allowances and reliefs.

In April 2001, new bereavement benefits for widows and widowers came into force. In addition to a non-taxable bereavement payment of £2,000, a taxable widowed parents' allowance payable to those with dependent children was introduced, as well as a taxable bereavement allowance (payable to qualifying persons aged over 45 for 52 weeks after a partner's death). See Chapter 21.

Home and possessions

Responsibility for a house or flat may need to be transferred to the name of another person. Relatives who were living with the deceased in rented accommodation should seek advice about their rights from a local Citizens Advice Bureau★ or solicitor.

Depending on his or her income and circumstances, a widow or widower may be eligible for housing benefit paid through the local authority to assist with rent or council tax. Leaflets GL16 *Help with Your Rent*, GL17 *Help with Your Council Tax* and GL18 *Help from the Social Fund* from the DWP Publications Orderline★ give details; alternatively, visit *www.dwp.gov.uk*.

It is necessary to inform certain parties about the death:

- the Inland Revenue, via your local tax office
- insurance or pension companies
- any hospital where the deceased had been receiving treatment
- the family doctor (if not already aware of the death)
- any employer or trade union
- any teacher or college
- the Post Office, to redirect mail if necessary
- the Social Services department, if home help and/or meals on wheels were provided; return loaned aids or appliances.

If the telephone was in the name of the deceased, the telephone company should be notified, and the service transferred to another name or terminated. A request should be made for the account up to the time of death to be rendered, so that the debt can be paid from the estate. Similarly, requests should be made to gas and electricity suppliers for meters to be read and accounts submitted; these accounts must also be transferred to another name if necessary.

Any library books, records, cassettes and video tapes should be returned to the respective libraries. If a house or flat has to be cleared, any furniture not required can be sold to a local dealer or put in an auction sale; a number of second-hand or antique dealers offer house clearance services – see local advertisements or *Yellow Pages*. The agreement should ensure that the house is left completely empty, and clean. Sometimes there will be an urgent need for cleaning of floors, carpets, bedding, furniture or curtains. Specialist contract cleaners offer such a service: again, see the local telephone book or *Yellow Pages*; funeral directors can often advise.

Local charity shops are glad to receive saleable items, although they must normally be delivered to the charity concerned at the donor's expense. If the local authority refuse department has to make a special collection, a charge may be made for this service. Second-hand clothing dealers are one way to get rid of unwanted items, but very little will be offered for them. Check all pockets, bags, cases etc. before disposing of them. Other unwanted possessions can also be advertised for sale locally, offered to a dealer or second-hand shop, or given to a charity. You should be careful when disposing of items to ensure a fair price is realised and specialist advice should be sought for the disposal of antiques or collections.

Paperwork

Inevitably there is some paperwork that will need to be dealt with when someone dies. The deceased's medical card, if available, should be taken to the registrar when registering the death. A rail season ticket should be taken to the station where it was issued, together with proof of death or probate, and a refund claimed. London Underground or bus season tickets may be surrendered at any Underground station, or posted to Transport for London★ or London Buses★. A refund may be made from the last day of use if a death certificate is produced, otherwise from the date of surrender. Refunds are made to the widow or widower; an executor may claim the refund on production of proof of probate or letters of administration, or on producing a solicitor's letter authorising payment.

Passports should be returned to the Passport Office★, or to any of the regional passport offices, together with a letter of explanation. If requested, passports will be returned after cancellation. Joint passports must be suitably amended by the Passport Office.

If the deceased owned a car, once the new ownership of the car has been settled, the top part of the registration document should be given to the new owner/keeper, and the bottom part sent to the Driver and Vehicle Licensing Agency (DVLA)*, so that the change of ownership can be recorded and a new registration document issued. The deceased person's driving licence should be returned to the DVLA and the car insurance company should be notified immediately. You may be able to claim a refund of some of the insurance premium that has been paid minus an administration fee.

If a widow, widower or partner is now the sole occupant of the house or flat, a rebate on council tax should be applied for.

For all other insurance policies in the name of the deceased, the relevant companies should be notified, the policies cancelled or amended, and any appropriate refunds claimed.

Any NHS equipment, for example, wheelchairs or hearing aids, should be returned to the NHS.

Claiming money due

Clubs and associations to which the dead person belonged should be told of the death and any unwanted subscriptions cancelled. There may be a refund to claim on unexpired memberships.

To claim on a life insurance policy, send the policy to the company together with the death certificate. A policy made 'in trust' for the widow/widower or other named beneficiary bypasses probate, and payment can be made to the beneficiary straight away. In all other cases, payment may be delayed until probate is granted. If this is more than two months after the date of death, the insurance company must add interest from then until the payment is made.

A number of employers have a life insurance scheme that pays out a lump sum on the death of an employee. And most company pension schemes provide either a cash sum or a pension (sometimes both) for dependants. Check with the last or current employer.

Various societies, professional bodies, trade unions and ex-service organisations run benevolent schemes for the dependants of their members or of people who qualify. The bereaved person should get in touch with the secretary of organisations the deceased belonged to to find out more.

Chapter 21

Pensions and other state benefits

Following the death of a spouse or close relative, you may become eligible for certain payments from the state.

The Department for Work and Pensions (DWP)★ administers all Social Security benefits. Explanatory leaflets for different categories of people – for example, on bereavement benefits – are available without charge at any local Social Security office or Jobcentre Plus office (*www.jobcentreplus.gov.uk*). A list of some relevant leaflets is given on pages 172–3. It is crucial to note that these leaflets are updated at irregular intervals and the information contained in them may change considerably from one edition to another; new leaflets are also produced. Please see the important note at the end of this chapter, and ensure that you always have the latest edition of the leaflet you want. You can ask the DWP or your local Social Security office if all the information in it is correct and up to date.

Some benefits are paid only to the dependants of those who had paid, or had credited to them, National Insurance contributions during their lifetime.

You are not expected to know what contributions have been paid or credited when you apply for any benefits. The Inland Revenue Contributions Office keeps records of everyone's contributions.

The number of contributions required varies according to the type of benefit claimed. When the number of contributions does not qualify for the full amount of certain benefits, a reduced rate may be paid.

If you need to find out more about claiming any benefits after someone has died abroad, write to the International Pension Centre★ of the DWP.

Help with funeral expenses

If you do not have enough money to pay for the funeral, and you or your partner are getting Income Support, income-based Jobseeker's Allowance, Pension Credit, Housing Benefit, Child Tax Credit (at a rate higher than the family element), Working Tax Credit (where a disabled worker is included in the assessment) or Council Tax Benefit, you may be able to get a Funeral Payment from the Social Fund to help with the cost. The decision is based on *your* financial circumstances, not those of the person who died. If you qualify for a payment from the Social Fund, your savings are no longer taken into consideration.

It is considered reasonable for you to pay for the cost of the funeral if you are the partner of the person who has died, or if you are a close relative or friend of the person if they did not have a partner. If the person who has died has a surviving parent or adult children who are not receiving any of the qualifying benefits and have savings above the threshold, the DWP will normally consider it reasonable for that person/those people to pay for the cost of the funeral. You should check if the deceased made any arrangements to pay for their funeral.

The Social Fund will make provision for up to £700 towards the funeral director's fees, which must include provision of a simple coffin and gown, removal of the deceased from the place of death to the funeral director's premises (up to a distance of 50 miles), and church, minister's and organist's fees. The funeral director's fees will probably amount to more than this, in which case the person arranging the funeral is responsible for paying anything above this amount. You can claim a Funeral Payment at any time after the person's death and up to three months after the date of the funeral.

In addition to the payment of £700 towards the fees of the funeral director, minister, organist and church, payment will be made for the cremation fee at a local crematorium (including the medical referee's fee), and the cost of any necessary doctors' certificates and the cost of removing a pacemaker.

If the funeral involves burial rather than cremation, the payment will, in addition to the £700, cover fees for the purchase of a new grave with exclusive right of burial (or fees for the reopening of an existing grave), interment fees and the gravedigger's fees. The reasonable cost of a journey either to arrange or to attend the funeral will be covered, but not both.

The Social Fund will not pay for newspaper announcements, the burial of cremated remains (ashes), religious requirements (such as taking the coffin into church the day before the funeral), memorials or flowers (unless there is money available from the balance of the £700 after all necessary fees have been paid).

How much you get from the Social Fund also depends on certain other funds which become available following the death, such as a life insurance policy, and any other money which is available for the funeral from other sources. If the person who died had a pre-paid funeral plan, payment from the Social Fund will be paid only for those necessary elements of the funeral not covered by the plan. A funeral payment made by the Social Fund will have to be paid back from the estate of the person who has died, should there be any money available. The law requires that funeral expenses must be paid before anything is paid from the estate. The home occupied by the partner of the person who has died, or personal possessions left to relatives, are not counted as part of the estate. You can find out more about funeral payments from the Social Fund in leaflet SB16 *A Guide to the Social Fund*.

Claims should be made on Form SF200, available from the Social Security office or funeral directors or downloaded from the DWP website (*www.dwp.gov.uk*), which should be accompanied by a copy of the funeral director's account. Completed forms must be sent to one of the DWP offices dealing with Social Fund claims, or taken to the local Social Security or Jobcentre Plus office. Pre-paid envelopes may be supplied with the SF200 pack, but are also obtainable from post offices. Currently, claims must be made within three months of the funeral.

It is important to check current arrangements with the Social Fund office at the local Social Security or Jobcentre Plus office, preferably before finalising funeral arrangements.

Bereavement benefits

There are three benefits that you may be entitled to if your husband or wife dies. These new benefits were introduced in April 2001 and replaced widow's allowance, widowed mother's allowance and widow's pension. To qualify for the benefits your husband or wife must have paid the required number of National Insurance (NI) contributions – your own NI contributions do not count. These new benefits are available to both widows and widowers. Previously, only women were eligible for bereavement benefits.

You need to have been married at the time of death to qualify – you will not be entitled to claim if you are divorced. You also lose your entitlement if you remarry or live with someone else as husband and wife as if you are married to them.

You can make a claim for bereavement benefits on Form BB1, available from any Social Security office or from the DWP★. Leaflet GL14 is also available from the DWP and is a basic guide to benefits and tax for women and men who have been widowed. Both documents can be downloaded from the DWP website. You will need to complete details of your marriage, pension and any dependent children on the form. To qualify you will need to send the death certificate, your birth certificate and marriage certificate, birth certificates for dependent children and your spouse's retirement pension order book with Form BB1.

You should claim the bereavement benefits as soon as possible to make sure you do not lose any of the benefits. Payments cannot normally be backdated for more than three months from the date of the application. Claimants should not delay if they are waiting for probate, which may take several months, but make an initial claim as soon as possible. When you make the application you can choose how any benefits are paid – either with a book of weekly orders or straight into a bank account.

Benefits are reviewed by the government at least once a year and benefits and qualifying conditions have been changed at short notice. The current amounts for the benefits described in the following pages are given on page 171. However, it is important to check the current position at your local Social Security or Jobcentre Plus office.

Bereavement payment

This is a tax-free payment of £2,000 paid to you as soon as you are widowed. However, it is payable only if your late husband or wife was not entitled to the state retirement pension when he or she died, or you were under the state pension age when your husband or wife died. You will not receive this payment if you are receiving a state pension.

Widowed parent's allowance

This is a taxable weekly benefit. It includes:

- a basic allowance for you
- an allowance for each of your dependent children
- additional State Earnings Related Pension (SERPS) if you qualify.

You are eligible for widowed parent's allowance if you have a child who qualifies for child benefit or you are expecting your late husband's baby. Your late spouse must also have met the NI contribution requirements, or his or her death must have been caused by his or her job. If you are a widower whose wife died before the introduction of widowed parent's allowance, you can still claim this allowance, provided you meet the entitlement conditions. Widowed parent's allowance will be paid for as long as you have a child under 16 (or under 19 if the child is in full-time education).

Bereavement allowance

This is a taxable weekly benefit paid for 52 weeks after your husband or wife dies, if you are aged 45 or over. Your late spouse must have met the required NI contributions. This replaces widow's pension. However, you will not get this bereavement allowance if you are entitled to widowed parent's allowance.

Married couple's allowance

Married couple's allowance was abolished with effect from April 2000. You will be able to claim only if the person who dies was born before 6 April 1935 (i.e. if the deceased was 65 before 6 April 2000). If you think you might be entitled to married couple's allowance, contact the Inland Revenue★.

If your wife dies, you can continue to receive the married couple's allowance for the whole of the tax year during which your wife dies. If part or all of the allowance had been allocated to your wife, you can have any unused part transferred to you.

War widow's pension

A widow whose husband had been in the armed forces should contact the Veterans Agency Helpline★, explaining the circumstances fully, and asking if she is entitled to a war widow's pension.

State Earnings Related Pensions (SERPS)

Previously, if a married person died who was entitled to a State Earnings Related Pension, the widow or widower could receive 100 per cent of his or her pension entitlement. From 6 October 2002 the government reduced this entitlement, and it will eventually be reduced to 50 per cent.

If a married person who dies after 6 October 2002 reached state pension age before that date, the widow or widower will still receive 100 per cent of his or her SERPS. Widows or widowers of people who reach state pension age after 5 October 2002 but before 6 October 2010 will receive between 60 per cent and 90 per cent of their spouse's SERPS. The exact amount will depend on when, in this period, the married person reaches state pension age. Widows or widowers of people who reach state pension age on or after 6 October 2010 will receive up to 50 per cent of their spouse's SERPS when they die.

The SERPS is paid in addition to any state retirement pension that is payable, and is now called the State Second Pension.

Other state benefits

If your income and savings are below certain levels you may be able to claim benefits to top up your income. Advice can be obtained from agencies such as the Citizens Advice Bureau★, as well as Social Security or Jobcentre Plus offices.

Income Support

If you don't work, or work for less than 16 hours a week, and your savings total less than £8,000, you can claim Income Support (known as Minimum Income Guarantee if you are over 60) if your weekly income is below a specified amount. This varies depending on your circumstances, i.e. your age, whether you have dependent children and, if so, how old they are, whether you have a disability or suffer from a chronic illness, whether you have a mortgage to pay and so on – see page 171.

Child Tax Credit and Working Tax Credit

From April 2003, Children's Tax Credit, Working Families Tax Credit and Disabled Person's Tax Credit were replaced by two new credits: the Child Tax Credit and Working Tax Credit. To receive one or both credits you need to claim via the Inland Revenue website★, or by phoning (0845) 300 3900 and asking for claim form TC600.

The new tax credit system may seem complicated – but do not be put off. You will not get them unless you apply for them. For more information, see the Inland Revenue website.

Child Tax Credit
This is a tax credit for people with children up to 16 years old (or under 19 if in full-time education). It is based on joint income and is payable to married couples or a man and woman or same-sex couple living together, in addition to child benefit. You do not have to be working to claim child tax credit. How much you receive depends on your income and the ages or disability of your children.

Working Tax Credit
This is a tax credit to top up the earnings of people on low incomes, including those who do not have children. There are extra amounts if you have a disability, pay for childcare or are over 50.

Pension Credit
Pension Credits are a new system for topping up pensioners' incomes. People aged 60 or over could claim extra money to guarantee them a minimum income. People over 65 who have modest savings or investments, or income from a second pension or annuity, may also be entitled to extra money. To apply, contact the Pension Service★.

Child Benefit
If you are bringing up a child, you can claim Child Benefit even if you are not the parent. Child Benefit is not affected by income or savings, and you need to claim in your name for each child under 16 or 19 if in full-time education.

Health costs
If you are claiming Income Support, Income-based Jobseeker's Allowance, Pension Credit or Working Tax Credit, you may be able to get help with health costs. If not, you may get help through the NHS low income scheme★.

Housing Benefit and Council Tax Benefit

If your savings are less than £16,000 and your income is below a certain amount (which varies according to your circumstances), you may be able to claim Housing Benefit to help you pay your rent and Council Tax. Claim forms and information are available from local council offices, for example leaflets GL16 *Help with Your Rent* and GL17 *Help with Your Council Tax*. All these are obtainable from the Social Security, DWP and Jobcentre Plus.

Jobseeker's Allowance

If you are unemployed, over 18 and less than 65 for men and 60 for women, capable of, available and actively seeking work you may be eligible to receive Jobseeker's Allowance. If enough National Insurance contributions have been paid, you may be able to get Contribution-based Jobseeker's Allowance; if not, you may be eligible for Income-based Jobseeker's Allowance (see page 172). For further information, see leaflet IR41, available from the Inland Revenue or Jobcentre Plus.

Guardian's Allowance

A person who takes an orphaned child into the family may be entitled to a Guardian's Allowance (see page 171). Although the payment is called a Guardian's Allowance, it is not necessary to assume legal guardianship to qualify. Usually the allowance is paid only when both parents are dead, but it can sometimes be paid after the death of one parent – for instance, where the other is missing or cannot be traced or is detained in prison or hospital, or where the parents were divorced (and certain conditions apply). The allowance is not awarded unless one of the child's parents was born in the UK or had been resident in the UK for a specified length of time, or is a national or member of a family of an EU country and insured under UK Social Security legislation. It is paid only if the guardian qualifies for child benefit for the child.

Claims for the allowance should be made on Form BG1, obtainable from the DWP or Jobcentre Plus. A claim should be made straight away as you may lose your benefit if you delay (it can be backdated only for up to three months or to the date of the award of Child Benefit).

National Insurance benefits: amounts

The 2005–06 weekly amounts payable for the benefits described in the preceding pages are as follows (unless otherwise stated). DWP leaflet **GL23** should be consulted for relevant updates.

Bereavement benefit

bereavement payment (lump sum)	£2,000
widowed parent's allowance	£82.05
bereavement allowance (standard rate)	£82.05

Income Support

The weekly *personal allowances* are:

aged under 18 (usual rate if eligible)	£33.85
aged under 18 (in special circumstances, if eligible)	£44.50
aged 18 to 24	£44.50
aged 25 or over	£56.20
couple (both aged 18 or over)	£88.15

Where one or both partners are aged under 18, their personal allowance will depend on their situation:

lone parents aged 16 to 17	£33.85
lone parents aged 16 to 17 in special circumstances	£44.50
lone parents aged 18 and over	£56.20

plus for each dependent child aged up to 16 or 18:

from birth until day before 19th birthday	£43.88

Guardian's Allowance

for each child who qualifies	£11.85
	(2004–05)

Jobseeker's Allowance

Contribution-based Jobseeker's Allowance:

person aged 16 to 17	£33.85
person aged 18 to 24	£44.50
person aged 25 or over	£56.20

Income-based Jobseeker's Allowance:

Personal Allowances and Premiums follow the general pattern of payments as made for Income Support: for full information see leaflet **GL23**.

171

Application forms and leaflets

Form	Source	Function/title
SF200	Registrar, DWP, Social Security office or Jobcentre Plus	to claim payment for funeral expenses from the Social Fund
BB1	DWP, Social Security office or Jobcentre Plus	to claim bereavement benefits (Bereavement Payment, Widowed Parent's Allowance, Bereavement Allowance)
BG1	Inland Revenue	to claim Guardian's Allowance
WTC1	Inland Revenue	Child Tax Credit and Working Tax Credit – an introduction
WTC2	Inland Revenue	Child Tax Credit and Working Tax Credit – a guide
D49	DWP, Social Security office or Jobcentre Plus	What to do after a death in England and Wales
D49S	DWP, Social Security office or Jobcentre Plus	What to do after a death in Scotland
NP45	DWP, Social Security office or Jobcentre Plus	A guide to bereavement benefits
NP46	DWP, Pension Service	A guide to State pensions
GL14	DWP, Social Security office or Jobcentre Plus	Widowed? A basic guide to benefits and tax credits for women and men who have been widowers
GL16	DWP, Social Security office or Jobcentre Plus	Help with your rent – a basic guide to Housing Benefit
GL17	DWP, Social Security office or Jobcentre Plus	Help with your Council Tax – a basic guide to Council Tax Benefit
GL18	DWP, Social Security office or Jobcentre Plus	Help from the Social Fund
GL23	DWP, Social Security office or Jobcentre Plus	Social Security benefit rates
IR45	Inland Revenue	What to do about tax when someone dies
IRLIST	Inland Revenue	Catalogue of leaflets and booklets
PM1	DWP Pension Service	A guide to your pension options – summary of the pensions system and points to think about
PM2	DWP, Pension Service	State pensions – your guide
PM3	DWP, Pension Service	Occupational pensions – your guide

PM4	DWP, Pension Service	Personal pensions – your guide
PM5	DWP, Pension Service	Self-employed
PM6	DWP, Pension Service	Pensions for women
CA09	Inland Revenue	National Insurance contributions for widows and widowers
RR2	DWP, Social Security office or Jobcentre Plus	A guide to Housing Benefit and Council Tax Benefit
IS20	DWP, Social Security office or Jobcentre Plus	A guide to Income Support
SB16	DWP, Social Security office or Jobcentre Plus	A guide to the Social Fund
WPA (leaflet 1)	DWP, Pension Service	Notes about War Disablement and and War Widows' pensions
WFPL1	DWP, Pension Service or Jobcentre Plus	Guide to winter fuel payments
HC1	DWP, Social Security office or Jobcentre Plus	Help with health costs

Websites
The following websites provide helpful information and also give up-to-date amounts for the benefits and allowances described in this chapter.

Department for Work and Pensions *www.dwp.gov.uk*
Inland Revenue *www.inlandrevenue.gov.uk*
Jobcentre Plus *www.jobcentreplus.gov.uk*
The Pension Service *www.pensionservice.gov.uk*

The government, the DWP and the Inland Revenue may make substantial changes to benefits and the qualifications for them at short notice. The information given here is accurate at the time of writing (February 2005), but if you are considering claiming any benefits or tax credits, it is very important that you contact your local Social Security office, Jobcentre Plus office, the DWP or Inland Revenue as soon as possible to get accurate and up-to-date information and advice. You should also make sure you have the latest edition of any leaflet, and ask if anything has changed since it was published. You may lose some benefits if you do not do this.

Chapter 22

Before your own death

Many people, when faced with the unfamiliar experience of having to arrange a funeral, find their task complicated because they do not have a grasp of the necessary details or know the wishes of the person who has died. A printed form, *Instructions for My Next of Kin and Executors Upon My Death*, is available from Age Concern England★ on receipt of a stamped, self-addressed envelope. Multiple copies can be obtained for 25p each. On this form, you can put down details about yourself which may be useful when your death is being registered (such as your place of birth, National Insurance number, details of parents and spouse/s), and provide information about your possessions, insurance policies and employer/s. Spaces are included for the names and addresses of relevant people such as your solicitor, bank manager, accountant and tax inspector. You can say on it where you keep important documents, not only your will, but birth certificate, marriage certificate, deeds of house, certificates, savings account books. Your wishes regarding your funeral can also be recorded on the form. Some funeral directors will also provide a free Personal Record File or similar document.

Make sure that your family or whoever you live with, or your executors, know about such forms and where they are kept.

The Age Concern form and others similar are not intended to take the place of a will; you are strongly advised to make a will even if you do not own very much.

The property of a person who dies intestate (that is, without leaving a valid will) is divided among the family according to the intestacy rules; if he or she has no close relatives, it may all go to the Crown.

Wills and Probate, available from Which? Books★, explains how to make a will, what to say in it, how to have it witnessed, and what happens if there is no will.

The Central Wills Directory★ provides a database of will-holders, and for a small fee will register the details and location of a will.

It is quite customary to put into a will whether you wish your body to be cremated or buried, but it is important to let your family know because there may be a delay before the will is read.

Making your wishes about organ donation known

You should ensure that all the relevant parties are aware of your intentions.

The donor card

Anyone who would like any part of his or her body to be used to save or prolong someone's life should have their name entered on the NHS Organ Donor Register (see page 58). This can be done by contacting the NHS Organ Donor Registration Service★, or completing one of the small red and blue donor cards available at GPs' surgeries, hospitals, clinics, dispensing chemists, libraries and other public offices. You can now also register online at *www.uktransplant.org.uk*. This card should be carried with you at all times. It is important, however, to discuss your wishes with your nearest kin and your GP and let them know that you have signed a donor card as evidence of your willingness to let parts of your body be used for the treatment of others. If you go into hospital as an in-patient, be sure to tell the ward sister or other senior members of staff that you are a potential donor.

Eyes

Corneal donation alone can be considered when someone dies at home or in hospital after any illness. In this case it is important to let the GP or hospital know about your intentions.

If you specifically want the cornea of your eyes to be used, you can get in touch with the research grants administrator at the Royal National Institute for the Blind (RNIB)★. You will be sent a multi-organ donor card to sign and keep, a leaflet giving information on what is involved, and a letter with details of the appropriate hospital to be contacted in your area. For further details, see Chapter 7.

The body

Before expressing a formal wish that your whole body be used for anatomical examination and medical education, you should discuss the matter with your family and next of kin, and also tell your executors, because they will have to act quickly after you have died.

To make the arrangements, you should contact the professor of anatomy at your nearest medical school or HM Inspector of Anatomy★ at the Department of Health. In Scotland the Scottish Executive Health★ can provide information.

For information about brain donation, see page 61.

Requesting cremation

The majority of funerals now involve cremation, and most people make their relatives aware of their wishes in this respect. However, the belief that cremation is something unusual still lingers on in some parts of society, and some people need to be reassured that no special registration is required, nor is it necessary to join a special scheme or society. A note to executors or family on a plain piece of paper stating your intent is quite valid. There is no legal obligation on executors or next of kin to carry out the wishes of the deceased regarding the funeral, but it would be extremely unusual if they did not do so. If you do leave written instructions for friends or family, make sure that they know where these are to be found.

Paying for the funeral in advance

An increasing number of people decide to make provision for the payment of their own funeral in advance, sometimes after being obliged to pay for the funerals of close relatives. This can be done in a number of ways:

- by investing a sufficient sum of money in a building society
- by taking out a life insurance policy specifically related to funeral expenses
- by joining one of the friendly societies which pay out a lump sum when death occurs
- by taking out a pre-paid funeral plan.

The following titles from Which? Books* provide detailed information about investment and life insurance options: *Be Your Own Financial Adviser* and *Money in Retirement*.

Pre-paid funeral plans

Pre-paid funeral plans are becoming increasingly popular: under this type of scheme, individuals choose the kind of funeral they would prefer and pay for it in advance at a current or slightly reduced rate. At the time of death, all funeral expenses, however much they may have increased, will be paid for through the scheme. Some plans reserve the right to make extra charges if the cost of disbursements (such as cremation or burial fees) rises higher than the rate of inflation, while others guarantee disbursements for cremation plans only, with a guaranteed minimum payment towards the cost of burial. Pre-paid funeral plans may be appropriate if you are keen to ensure that your specific personal wishes regarding your funeral are carried out, or want to spare friends and relatives the task of organising and possibly paying for your funeral.

A number of pre-paid schemes are currently available, all offering a selection of funeral types and prices. Almost all the schemes offer at least three choices:

- **basic** A simple funeral service, covering all the funeral director's charges, including a coffin and all necessary disbursements for cremation. Burial, which is usually more expensive, may involve an extra charge
- **standard** This covers the funeral director's services as above, but will include a better-quality coffin, a limousine for mourners and other services
- **superior** A service as above but often including a solid wood coffin and two or more limousines.

Other schemes allow the client to choose a tailor-made funeral and specify all the details. Most schemes make a commitment to covering all of the costs, however much they may rise due to inflation, but may only promise a contribution towards the cost of burial, which is rising unpredictably due to pressure on cemetery space. In keeping with social trends most pre-paid funeral plans opt for cremation, but will make a sum equivalent to the cost of cremation available for funerals which opt for burial.

Ensuring standards

The scheme concerned should be checked carefully to ensure that the proceeds are safely invested in a trust fund with a nationally recognised trustee, such as one of the high-street banks or national insurance societies. Make sure that the scheme is affiliated to the National Association for Pre-paid Funeral Plans (NAPFP)★ or the Funeral Planning Council (FPC)★, which co-operate with the Office of Fair Trading to establish guidelines for the protection of clients.

In early 2000, the Treasury announced that providers of pre-paid funeral plans must be regulated directly by the Financial Services Authority unless their schemes met strict criteria for exemption. To qualify for exemption, schemes must either be backed by suitable insurance from an authorised insurance company or hold purchasers' money in a trust, which must provide:

- legal constitution under a trust deed
- trust funds that are legally separate from the plan provider
- independent trustees
- funds that can only be withdrawn from the trust to pay for the funeral or give refunds
- authorised independent investment managers who follow strict investment criteria
- accounts which are audited annually.

Any other plan provider will need to apply to the Financial Services Authority for authorisation, in which case its clients will be protected by the Financial Services and Markets Act. Both the NAPFP and the FPC meet the criteria for exemption, and have worked together to establish the Funeral Planning Authority (FPA)★ as a self-regulatory body.

The FPA has set industry standards supported by a Code of Practice which includes arrangements to protect clients' funds and ensure delivery of the funerals agreed upon and anticipated by clients. It also promotes a compensation scheme and dispute resolution procedures, and provides standards of information for customers and those who are marketing plans.

Choosing and paying into a plan

Treasury research indicates that approximately 250,000 pre-paid funeral plans have been sold in the UK. At the time of writing, at least ten different schemes were available in the UK including one organised by the National Association of Funeral Directors (NAFD)★. Several national charities including Age Concern★, Help the Aged★ and Cruse Bereavement Care★ operate their own pre-paid funeral plans. Leaflets and brochures explaining all the schemes are available from funeral directors, or by response to media advertisements.

Payment into schemes can be made either as a lump sum or by instalments. The lump-sum payment for the cheapest available scheme amounts to about £1,400 (2005), and should cover all the essential costs of the funeral. Essential costs consist of the total of the funeral director's charges, and basic costs for cremation or burial. Some plans guarantee to cover all costs for cremation, but will pay only a sum equivalent to cremation costs towards a funeral which involves burial. Basic funeral plans would not normally cover such things as newspaper announcements, flowers for the funeral, service sheets, catering, memorials and so on. Some schemes will make provision for such costs provided they are specified and extra payments are made at the time of arranging the plan. Essential funeral costs should be covered no matter how much prices may rise, but a careful examination of the small print is necessary before signing any document which commits you to payment.

Instalments are payable over a number of years, the amount of which varies according to the scheme chosen. Should death occur before the instalments are fully paid, a sum equal to the number of instalments due (less the interest that would have been charged) will need to be paid by the executors. It is normal for a funeral director (not necessarily the one ultimately consulted) to be chosen when taking out the plan; when death occurs, the plan administrators are informed, who then instruct the nominated funeral director to carry out the arrangements.

Pre-paid funeral plans are marketed under various names, according to the organisation which provides them. Normally, funeral directors are agents for only one scheme, and several sources should be investigated before a choice is made. Reputable schemes provide peace of mind for many, but the small print always needs to be examined.

Addresses

Many organisations exist to offer help and support to bereaved individuals and families. Details of some are provided below, along with those of other organisations mentioned in the text.

Age Concern England
Astral House, 1268 London Road
Norbury, London SW16 4ER
Tel: 020-8679 8000
Fax: 020-8765 7211
Information line: (0800) 009 966
Email: ace@ace.org.uk
Website: www.ageconcern.org.uk

Age Concern Funeral Plan
Tel: (0800) 731 0651

Age Concern Northern Ireland
3 Lower Crescent
Belfast BT7 1NR
Tel: 028-9024 5729
Fax: 028-9023 5497
Email: info@ageconcernni.org
Website: www.ageconcernni.org

Age Concern Scotland
113 Rose Street
Edinburgh EH2 3DT
Tel: 0131-220 3345
Fax: 0131-220 2779
Information line: (0800) 009 966
Email: enquiries@acscot.org.uk
Website:
www.ageconcernscotland.org.uk

Age Concern Wales
4th Floor, 1 Cathedral Road
Cardiff CF11 9SD
Tel: 029-2037 1566
Fax: 029-2039 9562
Email: enquiries@accymru.org.uk
Website: www.accymru.org.uk

Asian Funeral Service
209 Kenton Road
Harrow
Middlesex HA3 0HD
Tel: 020-8909 3737
Fax: 020-8909 3435

Association of Burial Authorities
Waterloo House
155 Upper Street
London N1 1RA
Tel: 020-7288 2522
Fax: 020-7288 2533
Email: aba@swa-pr.co.uk

Association of Charity Officers
Unicorn House
Station Close
Potters Bar EN6 3JW
Tel: (01707) 651777
Fax: (01707) 660477
Email: info@aco.uk.net
Website: www.aco.uk.net

Benefits Agency
Look in your local phone book

Bereavement Register
Tel: (0870) 600 7222

Britannia Shipping Company for Burial at Sea Ltd
Unit 3, The Old Sawmills
Hawkerland Road
Collaton Raleigh, Sidmouth,
Devon EX10 0HP
Tel: (01395) 568652

British Eye Research Foundation
Lincoln House
75 Westminster Bridge Road
London SE1 7HS
Tel: 020-7928 7743
Fax: 020-7928 7919
Email: info@berf.org.uk
Website: www.berf.org.uk

British Humanist Association
1 Gower Street
London WC1E 6HD
Tel: 020-7079 3580
Fax: 020-7079 3588
Email: info@humanism.org.uk
Website: www.humanism.org.uk

British Organ Donor Society (BODY)
Balsham
Cambridge CB1 6DL
Tel: (01223) 893636
Email: body@argonet.co.uk
Website: www.argonet.co.uk/body

Central Wills Directory
PO Box 108
East Grinstead
West Sussex RH19 2YY
Tel: (01342) 302602
Fax: (01342) 835226
Email: info@willsdirectory.com
Website: www.willsdirectory.com

Citizens Advice Bureau
Look in your local phone book

Commonwealth War Graves Commission
2 Marlow Road
Maidenhead
Berkshire SL6 7DX
Tel: (01628) 634221
Fax: (01628) 771208
Website: www.cwgc.org

Compassionate Friends
53 North Street
Bristol BS3 1EN
Helpline: (08451) 232304
Tel: (08451) 203785
Fax: (08451) 203786
Email: info@tcf.org.uk
Website: www.tcf.org.uk

Cremation Society of Great Britain
2nd Floor, Brecon House
16–16a Albion Place
Maidstone ME14 5DZ
Tel: (01622) 688292/3
Fax: (01622) 686698
Email: cremsoc@aol.com
Website: www.cremation.org.uk

Cruse Bereavement Care
Cruse House, 126 Sheen Road
Richmond TW9 1UR
Helpline: (0870) 167 1677
Tel: 020-8939 9530
Fax: 020-8940 7638
Email: info@crusebereavement
care.org.uk
Website: www.crusebereavement
care.org.uk

Department for Work and Pensions (DWP)
Correspondence Unit, Room 112
The Adelphi
1–11 John Adam Street
London WC2N 6HT
Tel: 020-7712 2171
Fax: 020-7712 2386
Website: www.dwp.gov.uk

Department of Health Publications
PO Box 777
London SE1 6XH
Tel: (08701) 555455
Email: doh@prolog.uk.com
Website www.dh.gov.uk

Driver and Vehicle Licensing Agency (DVLA)
Swansea SA1 1AA
Tel: (0870) 240 0009
Website: www.dvla.gov.uk

DWP Publications Orderline
Fax: (01253) 333254
Website: www.dwp.gov.uk

Foreign and Commonwealth Office (FCO)
Consular Division
Nationality and Passport Section
Old Admiralty Building
Whitehall, London SW1A 2AF
Tel: 020-7270 1500
Website: www.fco.gov.uk

Foundation for the Study of Infant Deaths (FSID)
11–19 Artillery Row
London SW1P 1RT
Helpline: (0870) 787 0554
Tel: (0870) 787 0855
Fax: (0870) 787 0725
Email: fsid@sids.org.uk
Website: www.sids.org.uk/fsid

Funeral Planning Authority (FPA)
Knellstone House
Udimore
Rye
East Sussex TN31 6AR
Tel: (0845) 601 9619
Email: info@funeralauthority.co.uk
Website: www.funeralplanning authority.com

Funeral Planning Council (FPC)
Melville House
70 Drymen Road
Bearsden, Glasgow G61 2RP
Tel: 0141-942 5855
Fax: 0141-942 2323
Email: mailbox@golden-charter.co.uk
Website: www.golden-charter.co.uk

General Register Office
PO Box 2
Southport
Merseyside PR8 2JD
Tel: (0845) 603 7788
Website: www.gro.gov.uk

General Register Office for Scotland
New Register House
3 West Register Street
Edinburgh EH1 3YT
Tel: 0131-314 4446
Fax: 0131-314 4400
Email: records@gro-scotland.gov.uk
Website: www.gro-scotland.gov.uk

Help the Aged
Head Office
207–221 Pentonville Road
London N1 9UZ
Tel: 020-7278 1114
Fax: 020-7278 1116
Email: info@helptheaged.org.uk
Website: www.helptheaged.org.uk

HM Inspector of Anatomy
Room 630, Department of Health
Wellington House
135–155 Waterloo Road
London SE1 8UG
Tel: 020-7972 4551
Fax: 020-7972 4791
Email:
karen.huscrof@doh.gsi.gov.uk

Home Office
Coroner's Section
Email: public.enquiries@home
office.gsi.gov.uk
Website: www.homeoffice.gov.uk

Inland Revenue
*Look in the phone book for your local tax
office or Inland Revenue Enquiry Centre.*
Website: www.inlandrevenue.gov.uk

INQUEST
89–93 Fonthill Road
London N4 3JH
Tel: 020-7263 1111
Fax: 020-7561 0799
Email: inquest@inquest.org.uk
Website: www.inquest.org.uk

Institute of Family Therapy
24–32 Stephenson Way
London NW1 2HX
Tel: 020-7391 9150
Fax: 020-7391 9169
Website: www.instituteoffamily
therapy.org.uk

International Pension Centre
Tyneview Park
Newcastle-upon-Tyne NE98 1BE
Tel: 0191-218 7777
Website:
www.thepensionservice.gov.uk

**Iris Fund for the Prevention of
Blindness**
See British Eye Research Foundation

**Jewish Bereavement Counselling
Service**
8–10 Forty Avenue
Wembley
Middlesex HA9 8JW
Tel: 020-8385 1874
Fax: 020-8385 1856
Email: jbcs@jvisit.org.uk
Website: www.jvisit.org.uk

Law Society of England and Wales
Law Society Hall
113 Chancery Lane
London WC2A 1PL
Tel: 020-7242 1222
Fax: 020-7831 0344
Website: www.lawsociety.org.uk

Law Society of Northern Ireland
Law Society House
98 Victoria Street
Belfast BT1 3JZ
Tel: 028-9023 1614
Fax: 028-9023 2606
Email: info@lawsoc-ni.org
Website: www.lawsoc-ni.org

Law Society of Scotland
26 Drumsheugh Gardens
Edinburgh EH3 7YR
Tel: 0131-226 7411
Fax: 0131-225 2934
Email: lawscot@lawscot.org.uk
Website: www.lawscot.org.uk

London Buses
Customer Service Centre
172 Buckingham Palace Road
London SW1W 9TN
Tel: (0845) 300 7000
Fax: 020-7918 3999
Email: customerservice@
tfl-buses.co.uk
Website: www.tfl.gov.uk/buses

Macmillan Cancer Relief Fund
89 Albert Embankment
London SE1 7UQ
Helpline: (0808) 808 2020
Email: cancerline@macmillan.org.uk
Website: www.macmillan.org.uk

Mailing Preference Service (MPS)
DMA House
70 Margaret Street
London W1W 8SS
Tel: 020-7291 3310
Email: mps@dma.org.uk
Website: www.mpsonline.org.uk

Miscarriage Association
c/o Clayton Hospital
Northgate, Wakefield
West Yorkshire WF1 3JS
Tel: (01924) 200799
Fax: (01924) 298834
Email: info@miscarriageassociation.
org.uk
Website: www.miscarriageassociation.
org.uk

**National Association for Pre-paid
Funeral Plans (NAPFP)**
618 Warwick Road
Solihull
West Midlands B91 1AA
Tel: 0121-711 1343
Fax: 0121-711 1351
Email: enquiries@napfp.co.uk
Website: www.napfp.co.uk

**National Association of Funeral
Directors (NAFD)**
618 Warwick Road
Solihull
West Midlands B91 1AA
Tel: (0845) 230 1343
Fax: 0121-711 1351
Email: info@nafd.org.uk
Website: www.nafd.org.uk

**National Association of Memorial
Masons**
27a Albert Street
Rugby
Warwickshire CV21 2SG
Tel: (01788) 542264
Fax: (01788) 542276
Email: enquiries@namm.org.uk
Website: www.namm.org.uk

National Association of Widows
48 Queens Road
Coventry CV1 3EH
Tel: 024-7663 4848
Email: office@nawidows.org.uk
Website: www.nawidows.org.uk

**National Council for Voluntary
Organisations**
Regent's Wharf
8 All Saints Street
London N1 9RL
Tel: 020-7713 6161
Email: ncvo@ncvo-vol.org.uk
Website: www.ncvo-vol.org.uk

National Funerals College
Professor Malcolm Johnson
Chairman
Leyton House
6 Warwick Road
Bristol BS6 6HE
Tel: 0117-973 0045
Fax: 0117-330 6162
Email: malcolm.johnson@
bristol.ac.uk

National Secular Society
25 Red Lion Square
London WC1R 4RL
Tel/Fax: 020-7404 3126
Email: kpw@secularism.org.uk
Website: www.secularism.org.uk

Natural Death Centre
6 Blackstock Mews
Blackstock Road
London N4 2BT
Tel: (0871) 288 2098
Fax: 020-7354 3831
Email: ndc@alberyfoundation.org
Website: www.naturaldeath.org.uk

NHS Low Income Scheme
Tel: (0845) 850 1166

NHS Organ Donor Register
UK Transplant (UKT)
Fox Den Road
Stoke Gifford
Bristol BS34 8RR
Tel: 0117-975 7575
Fax: 0117-975 7577
*The register deals with previously
registered donors*

**NHS Organ Donor Registration
Service**
Tel: (0845) 606 0400
Website: www.uktransplant.org.uk
*Contact the service to register as an organ
donor*

Oddfellows Friendly Society
Oddfellows House
40 Fountain Street
Manchester M2 2AB
Tel: 0800 028 1810
Website: www.oddfellows.co.uk

Parkinson's Disease Society
215 Vauxhall Bridge Road
London SW1V 1EJ
Tel: 020-7931 8080
Helpline: (0808) 800 0303
Fax: 020-7233 9908
Email: enquiries@parkinsons.org.uk
Website: www.parkinsons.org.uk

Passport Office
Tel: (0870) 521 0410 (*enquiry line*)
Email: info@passport.gov.uk
Website: www.passport.gov.uk
Call for details of your local office

The Pension Service
Tel: (0845) 606 0265
Website:
www.thepensionservice.gov.uk

Probate and Inheritance Tax
Helpline: (0845) 302 0900

Public Search Room
Family Records Centre
1 Myddleton Street
London EC1R 1UW
Tel: (0845) 603 7788
Email: certificate.services@
ons.gov.uk
Website: www.gro.gov.uk

Rationalist Press Association
1 Gower Street
London WC1E 6HD
Tel: 020-7436 1151
Fax: 020-7079 3588
Email:
webcontact@newhumanist.org.uk
Website: www.newhumanist.org.uk

Registrar General (Northern Ireland)
Oxford House
49–55 Chichester Street
Belfast BT1 4HL
Tel: 028-9025 2163
028-9025 2000 (*credit-card line*)
Website: www.groni.gov.uk

Registry of Shipping and Seamen
Tel: 029-2044 8800
Fax: 029-2044 8820
Email: rss@mcga.gov.uk

Retained Organs Commission
Website:
www.nhs.uk/retainedorgans

Roadpeace
PO Box 2579
London NW10 3PW
Tel: 020-8838 5102
(0845) 4500 355 (*support line*)
Email: info@roadpeace.org
Website: www.roadpeace.org
Support and information for those
bereaved by road death

Royal National Institute for the Blind
(RNIB)
105 Judd Street
London WC1H 9NE
Tel: 020-7388 1266
Helpline: (0845) 766 9999
Fax: 020-7388 2034
Email: helpline@rnib.org.uk
Website: www.rnib.org.uk

Samaritans
Helpline: (0845) 790 9090
Email: jo@samaritans.org
Website: www.samaritans.org
Look in your telephone book for local branch

Scottish Executive Health
St Andrews House
Regent Road
Edinburgh EH1 3DG
Tel: 0131-556 8400
Website: www.scotland.gov.uk

Sea Fisheries Inspectorate
Room 13, East Block
10 Whitehall Place
London SW1A 2HH
Tel: 020-7270 8328
Helpdesk: (0845) 933 5577
Fax: 020-7270 8345
Email: sfiadmin@defra.gsi.gov.uk
Website: www.defra.gov.uk

Society of Allied and Independent
Funeral Directors (SAIF)
3 Bullfields
Sawbridgeworth
Hertfordshire CM21 9DB
Tel: (0845) 230 6777
Fax: (01279) 726300
Email: info@saif.org.uk
Website: www.saif.org.uk

South Place Ethical Society
Conway Hall
25 Red Lion Square
London WC1R 4RL
Tel: 020-7242 8037/4
Fax: 020-7242 8036
Email: library@ethicalsoc.org.uk
Website: www.ethicalsoc.org.uk

Stillbirth and Neonatal Death Society
(SANDS)
28 Portland Place
London W1B 1LY
Tel: 020-7436 7940
Helpline: 020-7436 5881
Email: support@uk-sands.org
Website: www.uk-sands.org

Support after Murder and
Manslaughter (SAMM)
Cranmer House
39 Brixton Road
London SW9 6DZ
Tel: 020-7735 3838
Email: enquiries@samm.org.uk
Website: www.samm.org.uk

Transport for London
Windsor House
42–50 Victoria Street
London SW1 0TL
Tel: 020-7941 4500
Website: www.tfl.gov.uk

UK Transplant (UKT)
Information Executive
Fox Den Road
Stoke Gifford
Bristol BS34 8RR
Tel: 0117-975 7575
Fax: 0117-975 7577
Website: www.uktransplant.org.uk

Unrelated Live Transplant
Regulatory Authority (ULTRA)
Room 423
Wellington House
135–155 Waterloo Road
London SE1 8UG
Tel: 020-7972 4812
Fax: 020-7972 4790
Email: dhmail@doh.gsi.gov.uk
(please make clear your email is for
ULTRA)
Website:
www.advisorybodies.doh.gov.uk/ultra

Veterans Agency
Norcross
Blackpool FY5 3WP
Helpline: (0800) 169 2277
Email:
help@veteransagency.gsi.gov.uk
Website: www.veteransagency.
mod.uk

Which? Books
PO Box 44
Hertford X, SG14 1LH
Tel: (0800) 252100
Website: www.which.co.uk

Index